Through the Seasons with Jesus and Mary

AMY MOSBACHER

Kathy,
Keep the faith!
In Christ,
Amy Mosbacher

PAGE PUBLISHING, INC.
New York, NY

First originally published by Page Publishing, Inc. 2015

ISBN 978-1-68139-082-6 (pbk)
ISBN 978-1-68139-083-3 (digital)

Printed in the United States of America

To my mom and dad for giving me
such a great foundation. To my husband and
daughters, without whom I wouldn't have
learned all these lessons.

Most of all, to my Lord and His blessed mother
Mary for being my constant companions.

ACKNOWLEDGMENTS

I'd like to thank Fr. Fedor first of all for encouraging me for so long to put together this book. I'm sure he's saying "finally!" from his place up there in heaven. Thank you, Dana and Dee, for your multitude of prayers and phone calls that kept me sane. To everyone at Page Publishing who has helped with each step, thank you for making this book a reality. And above all for my family, especially my husband, who has cheered me on through all the ups, downs and crazy hours of creating a book, thank you!

An inspiration to families everywhere! Amy's book is a loving, truthful, and honest guide to how an ordinary Christian family confronts everyday problems. They grow personally and spiritually in truth-revealing moments as difficult events are dealt with among themselves and others. With self-respect and a great confidence in God, Amy searches for answers to puzzling moments in their lives. The considerations presented here provide valuable answers in handling challenges affecting faith and belief in a rapidly changing and complex society.

—Fr. Robert Fedor,
Diocese of Erie, Pennsylvania

CONTENTS

Lent

The Triduum

Easter

INTRODUCTION

Come. I want to tell you a story. From before recorded history began sprang an eternal love story, and it continues today. Taking it in all at once may be overwhelming if you're unfamiliar with it. We must be wooed in, perhaps a page at a time.

December begins the liturgical year of the church. What an odd time to begin a new year—the beginning of winter when the world is at its darkest. But then the church isn't guided by human rationality. She takes her cue from her Creator, from someone who can see beyond the present darkness to the light. I want to share that *someone* with you, so you also may know the joy and hope I have. What? How can I say joy and hope with the world drowning in chaos? Because the God who governs people and the laws of nature sees the whole picture and he knows what we need most. We need someone to hope in, someone who knows our hurts and suffers with us, someone who can pick us up, heal wounded hearts, and say we'll be okay. God sent us hope, and its name is Jesus.

Maybe you ask, who is God? Why should he be interested in anything I do? And why should I care? What does Jesus have to do with me? It's a strange God who, motivated by love, created humans with free will, so we could share his love and joy in return. But rather than share in our Father's plan, we pridefully wandered away from our Father through disobedience. In order to win our hearts back from the devil, God chose what we in our wisdom cannot understand: to become one of us, human, so we could hear his voice giving clear directions back to him, and then to die and rise again, opening the door that death closed.

Jesus is God speaking. Jesus said that he and God the Father are one and the same, and everything Jesus says comes from the Father. The Bible contains everything Jesus taught while on earth as well as the story of how people came to know God's love for them. His love for us is still a mystery, but the humility God exhibits in his desire for us to know him is evident. He doesn't force; rather, he invites. Let's explore the invitation using sacred scripture and the Tradition of the church, highlighting some of the holy days throughout the year. By giving some of my own experiences, I challenge you to ponder where, or if, God is in your life, and find your part in his story as well. It is there.

PROLOGUE

"Jesus asked him, 'What do you want me to do for you?'" (Luke 18: 40–41).

"They name him Wonder-Counselor, God-Hero, Father-Forever, Prince of Peace"(Is.9:5).

Holy, holy, holy is the Lord God almighty, who was, and who is, and who is to come...Worthy are you, Lord our God, to receive glory and honor and power, for you created all things; because of your will they came to be and were created. (Rev. 4:8, 11).

"Worthy is the Lamb that was slain to receive power and riches, wisdom and strength, honor and glory and blessing" (Rev. 5:12).

"I [am] the Alpha and the Omega, the beginning and the end" (Rev. 21:6).

"The Lord God formed man out of the clay of the ground and blew into his nostrils the breath of life, and so man became a living being" (Gen. 2:7).

"For you are dirt, and to dirt you shall return" (Gen. 3:19).

"What do you want me to do for you?" (Matt. 20:32).

"O Lord, our Lord, how awesome is your name through all the earth! You have set your majesty above the heavens" (Ps. 8:2).

"The Lord is in his holy temple; the Lord's throne is in heaven" (Ps. 11:4).

"All things came to be through him, and without him nothing came to be. What came to be through him was life, and this life was the light of the human race" (John 1:3–4).

"What are humans that you are mindful of them, mere mortals that you care for them?" (Ps. 8:5).

"Before I formed you in the womb I knew you, before you were born I dedicated you" (Jer.1:5).

"And the Word became flesh and made his dwelling among us…the glory as of the Father's only Son, full of grace and truth" (John 1:14).

"Jesus said to him…, 'What do you want me to do you for?'" (Mark 10:51).

"Jesus, looking at him, loved him" (Mark 10: 21).

What do you want me to do for you?" (Mark 10:51).

ADVENT AND CHRISTMAS

Mary's hands grew still over the baby garment she was sewing, and her eyes lifted, gazing into the distance. Her thoughts took her back to that day nearly nine months ago. The whole event still amazed her, and if not for the movements of the baby silently growing within she might have considered it a dream. The angel was beautiful beyond description, announcing to her words she never thought to hear, "Hail, favored one" (Luke 1:28). The message he gave was beyond belief, that she would carry a child who would be called the Son of the Most High God. She had no doubt in her mind when she agreed, for God was wisdom, and he knew what was best for her. She was amazed though that he had chosen her. She was no one. In her most daring thoughts, she'd hoped to one day serve the coming Messiah, but to be his mother? Well! Digesting this would take much prayer.

Joseph hadn't taken the news of her pregnancy very well. Although she knew God would protect her and his Son, Mary had asked God to surround her with angels when she broached the subject more because she needed courage. The disappointed look in Joseph's eyes had brought tears to her own. A light seemed to have gone out of him. He'd left the house, and Mary later heard from her mother that Joseph intended to divorce her. How she'd prayed that God would help him! And God had come through, sending Joseph an angel in a dream. Now Joseph considered her and his own position with wonder. Suddenly, he was the foster father, raising a child who claimed God as true Father and had a great destiny awaiting him. Could he do this? Both he and Mary prayed and prayed that they'd be up to this task. They prayed, and they waited.

When hope becomes human

At times it seems a ludicrous thing to speak to someone who is aching about hope. When, for whatever reason, their world is crashing down about them, their heart being rent in two and no light is seen in the distance, they might well believe that hope is a denial of reality and all that's left is the dreariness of life. If it weren't for Jesus, that would be true. But Jesus gives us a foretaste of our eternal life with God our Father.

Let's stop for a minute from the busyness of the season and consider the God who took on our humanness. God lives in us (whether we recognize it or not) because we're his creation. Over time we've forgotten how to listen to his voice and recognize his presence. In our world of thirty-second advertisements, the two-minute witness, and when five minutes is too long at a drive-through restaurant, we've lost the ability to look at a static picture for a longer length of time without being impatient. Can our brains, bombarded as they are with rapid images and noise, still focus on one thing long enough for its depth and meaning to penetrate our hearts and leave us with an appreciation for the thing? If we go to an art museum, how much time do we spend at a single picture before moving on? Unless we make time to come to God in our hearts, we won't leave ourselves open to receive the gift of prayer. We need to make time for him, whether we're busy working, playing, or even resting, and go to that place in our hearts where there is silence and let ourselves rest in his presence because he is always there (we just have to realize it). Prayer is simply the desire for God. Perhaps picking a verse from scripture will help us be still and know him better. It doesn't have to be long. For example, the last line of Proverbs 8:31 says, "And I found delight in the sons of men." The words are so few, but how potent! To think that our Lord in all his wisdom, holiness, and the beauty of heaven prefers and finds his delight in dwelling among his creatures here on earth. Don't just read the line and think, How very nice, but contemplate it and be overwhelmed by it! The pure God who created and knows us to be sinful still loves us so much that he wants to be with us even to enter our reality in time and take on our nature. He takes on the suffering that we created and, therefore, makes it holy. When we think about the grace he has given us and come to appreciate it, that's when we humble ourselves and fall down before him and truly cry out, "My Lord and my God!" Such is adoration. From that exuberance, we come once again to the quiet, grateful worship of God that leaves us in awe of him and his wonders.

DANCING IN THE DARKNESS

The quiet gives us a chance to breathe. Christmas and all surrounding holidays are hard on us for a multitude of reasons. But we who believe in God were given a lifeline, something to look forward to beyond and better than the current circumstances, something which helps us muddle through. The hope that we've been given also gives us patience because we know that these sufferings now are nothing compared to the joys of heaven. We can endure anything if we know he's waiting for us with open arms at the end. That's what confounds the world, how we can dance in this darkness with everything going wrong and still be joyful and hopeful.

God sends his hope to all of us, but we have the advantage. We have hindsight; we know the story of Jesus's life. For those who lived with Jesus and didn't know the future, events unfolded uncertainly. Constantly asking what's next? God sent his Son to one couple, very specifically, Mary and Joseph. Two thousand years ago an angel gave a simple salutation to a humble young girl who said yes. The plan was set in motion. The Holy Spirit came over Mary, and God's word was made flesh. Then she waited, her heart a mixture of joy and anxiety. What would Joseph think? How would she explain an unexpected pregnancy to her future husband? Holy Mary, pray for us when life doesn't go as planned. Pray for God's strength and courage to hold us up in trials and wisdom, so we make choices which will make our Father smile. Help us be aware of events working out naturally and especially when God intervenes, as he did with Joseph. Thank heavens for dreams! Instead of divorcing Mary as he'd planned, Joseph accepted her pregnancy as coming from God and took her into his home. Hardship walked with them from the beginning. Even two thousand years ago, people were sure to be counting on their fingers when the baby was born. They both probably endured looks of disapproval and whispered rumors. In their hearts, they knew the truth and let that carry them. The young couple fixed their eyes on God and started to prepare a home. After all the mystical happenings with angels and dreams, life took on practicality now. Mary made clothing, Joseph a cradle and maybe even toys for the baby. As they worked, they wondered, What would the baby look like? Their hearts beat a little faster in anticipation. Imagine, to be the mother (dared Mary even think of it?) of the God who created her. What would looking in his eyes be like? Perhaps she also had all sorts of advice from her own mother and other relatives on how to care for a baby. Like other pregnant women, a nesting period of ferocious house cleaning might have afflicted her. She probably couldn't do too much though, as she knew her child's special origin and that he'd be born in Bethlehem. Scripture said the Messiah would come from Bethlehem, and Mary and Joseph knew the scriptures as well as anyone of their day. Since they didn't live in Bethlehem, how exactly that was supposed to happen? They didn't know until news came of a census. Joseph's origins were from Bethlehem so, in obedience to the law, off they went. They didn't have plans for when they arrived, but they trusted God would take care of them. How much do we trust when we can't see the road ahead? Let's take our example from Mary and Joseph. Give thanks to God for the ways all of his plans are accomplished!

PREPARATIONS

Options abound in travel methods today. Often multihour car trips are swapped for more direct flight plans, or trains are filled with people hunched over books and phones. Media permeates the fabric of our lives, even when we try to escape it. Advent beckons us to a quieter place and a different kind of journey. Christmas is coming. Is Christmas only for gifts? Our world tries making us think that, but we know differently. As we journey around the Advent wreath, lighting candles, anticipating the birth of Jesus, let's quiet ourselves, pray, and make ready.

I remember when I was nine months pregnant. My doctor didn't let me go more than half an hour outside of town. Imagine Mary's apprehension at leaving home, family, and friends and traveling to an unknown place. How she trusted in God's providence and protection! I talked and sang to my babies the whole term, and I was so anxious to have them as the time drew near. No doubt Mary did the same with a protective hand over her belly. Such closeness. At no other time would Jesus be so near her heart. At this point, she didn't know what it was like to have a child—to have her heart live on the outside of her body. She didn't know the joys and sorrows of motherhood, much less those belonging to the mother of the Messiah. Now she was still dreaming of the day when she could look into his eyes as reflections of her own and say, "Flesh of my flesh, heart of my heart, I love you." Oh, what a mother would do to protect her baby! Mary and Joseph traveled by foot or sometimes by donkey. Either way exhausted Mary with the load she carried inside her. We don't know if Joseph had any relatives in town, but if he did, they didn't welcome him. The knot in his stomach moved up to his throat the longer they looked for a place. He wept when God provided shelter in relief, gratitude, and perhaps disappointment in what he himself couldn't provide. Joseph glanced at his wife, reassured by her calmness and acceptance of the surroundings. He pulled himself together and started gathering wood for a fire. Mary swallowed. The confidence Joseph exuded calmed her as she looked around the cave. Not quite what she pictured for having a baby. The dank air was musty and smelled of animals and hay. The hay was good; it reminded her of home. She sighed. If this is what God wanted, then okay. She prayed and drew strength from Joseph as he busied himself settling them in. Was everything ready for the baby? Did she have enough blankets for this cold? Mary rustled through their packs anxiously, wondering if she had done enough. He would come soon.

Are we ready? Christmas will come soon. The house is ready with pine boughs, tiny lights, and smells of cookies lingering in the air. Presents wrapped under the tree wait to bring smiles to their receivers. All seems ready, but have we prepared our hearts as well?

As much as we anticipate Christmas, how much more God anticipates coming to us! Sometimes the days just fly by, and we don't feel we've done enough to prepare spiritually. Perhaps then we think, Oh, Jesus would never come to me anyway. I've done this horrible thing or that, or what would he want with me. Don't think that way! God doesn't dwell on past mistakes; he's God of the here and now. While hours spent in prayer may be nice and certainly do help in our journey to God, one quick glance and a thought of him will cause Jesus to come rushing to us, saying, "Yes, I will come and live in your heart and love you, and it will be you and I together..." All we have to do is ask. Don't worry or despair. Advent is all about hope when we can ask Jesus to come into our hearts regardless of the past. We know that his presence will heal all wounds. Isn't getting to know Jesus the best gift we can give ourselves?

THE WORD WAS MADE FLESH

Inky blackness covered the land the night heaven touched earth, but in a rocky cave used for a stable outside Bethlehem, "the light shines in the darkness, and the darkness has not overcome it" (John 1:5). When the angels' songs faded, a baby's squall broke the stillness. He was hungry and cold. What joy Mary and Joseph found, cradling Jesus in their arms! They gazed at the infant, looking at their God who'd come willingly into their lives. How overwhelming for Mary, to look on the face of her baby, her God, and see her own features! Oh, the joy of that meeting between God and man, the beginning of an eternal union.

In fields surrounding the outskirts of town, a tired shepherd walked among his sheep. What they were anxious about, he couldn't tell, but they wouldn't lie down. His gaze strayed to his fellow shepherds as they took their turn dozing. He envied them their rest, but his watch would be over soon enough. At least the sheep weren't running about, but just standing quietly, like they were waiting. As the boy turned to make another round, he froze. There before him was a being, glowing, radiating joy, bathed in the glory of God. The shepherd cried out and fell to the ground, burying his face in the grass. "Do not be afraid!" He raised his head and saw the other shepherds, awoken by his cry, also crouching low. The angel lifted his arms and said, "I proclaim to you good news of great joy that will be for all the people. For today in the city of David a savior has been born for you who is Messiah and Lord. And this will be a sign for you: you will find an infant wrapped in swaddling clothes and lying in a manger" (Luke 2:11–12).

Then the sky appeared filled with angels all singing of God's glory, and light fell from each of them like glitter, falling to the ground. After they'd gone, the shepherds agreed to go and find the baby the angel spoke about. They discovered the rocky cave sheltering Joseph and Mary and the baby just as they were told, and understanding filled their hearts. They were the first to see him that night, and their enthusiasm spilled into the town. Crowds of people gathered before the entrance, lining up to come before the small baby. Gifts were brought and words of hope exchanged. God touched the world that night, and people left the holy family feeling a little lighter than when they came. As for Mary and Joseph, they looked at each other and then the baby, their eye's following the lines of people streaming forth from the town, and they held all these things in their hearts.

DISCOVERING LIGHT

December is literally, and recently figuratively as well, a very dark time. It's the darkest month. Economic recession and political turbulence rock society, and we live in a culture of death. Add any personal turmoil to this, and it could be downright depressing. We so need Jesus to be our pillar of strength, our anchor to ride through the storm. But if we don't know him, how can we know the hope he offers? I can write and teach till I'm blue in the face, but I can't give you the hope that Jesus gives me. Only he can do that, only he can give the joy that comes from loving him. Ask God for the desire to know him better. Ask for the desire to read the Bible. It's God who places that desire in you, and he gives generously. If you don't know where to start, pick up the Bible and find the gospels. There you can find Jesus's words of reassurance, his looks of love for you. Discover that he walks with us. He's there, drudging through the mud and pain with us and experiencing everything we feel, and he gives us hope that this too will pass. In the end, there is only he and you, you and him, and together there is joy. Our Father so wants us to live our lives with him that he came in human form to be with us so that we'd know there is more than this present life and that his love is awaiting us. When I was ten, I spent quite a bit of time sneaking into my parents' room because there was a book on their shelves I loved to read. I always felt guilty trespassing, but the allure of that book was irresistible. What drew me to that clandestine operation was none other than the Jerusalem Bible. I don't know what it was that pulled me. That particular version is the most poetic translation, but I find it hard to believe at ten I knew anything about good or bad translations. All I knew was I was lost in those pages of God's love song to me, and they filled the yearning I had. The stories of Jesus were far more interesting than the rest of the New Testament, but what also caught my attention was the Psalms. My favorite was Psalm 42:6: "Why are you downcast, my soul; why do you groan within me? Wait for God, whom I shall praise again, my savior and my God." I actually wrote it down on a slip of paper and carried it around with me everywhere I went. One reason I liked the verse was probably because I didn't have many friends at school (I admit I was the goat of the class) and often spent time alone. I didn't realize what a huge grace God was giving me at the time, inspiring a ten-year-old to spend so much time reading the Bible. Yet that was what gave me strength to endure not only grade school but the disintegration of my family in the years ahead. There were times when I surely would have given up save for the fact that I knew someday I would be happy again in heaven with him. Jesus gave me hope that the present situation wouldn't last, that there was light in the darkness. No matter how dark it got, I could always hold onto that Light, Jesus.

LET THERE BE PEACE

The Catholic Church teaches that "the home is the first school of Christian life" and there "one learns endurance and the joy of work, fraternal love, generous—even repeated—forgiveness, and above all divine worship in prayer and the offering of one's life" (Catholic Church 1994, 1657). In a perfect world perhaps every home would be that, but we don't live in a perfect world. So it seems that even the broken homes must resemble the church, especially now with all the scandals and dissension. On a grander scale, perhaps these homes even resemble the world at large, or more likely, the world resembles the broken homes. How can we have peace between governments if we can't even have peace within families? As Pope St. John Paul II said in his World Day of Peace message in 2002, there can be "no peace without justice, no justice without forgiveness." So we can pray for peace between countries all we want, but unless we start with ourselves and those around us, it just isn't going to happen. Well then, is there any hope? we ask. I look at the situation in Iraq, the bombings in Turkey, unrest in Africa and so many places, the moral decline of Europe and America, and around me I look at my parents' own shattered home from which I hail. To this all, I say, yes, there is hope, and its name is Jesus. To forgive is a supremely hard act to make, and if it weren't for Jesus's forgiveness, probably wouldn't happen at all. He broke the cycle of violence by not striking back. Instead, he came into a world full of hurting people who were longing for healing, longing for a savior's touch. He was born in poverty, and his life was anything but peaceful. He experienced the world in joy and sorrow, and that's how we are meant to know life as well, in joy and sorrow. Finally, at the end of his life, he said, "Peace I leave with you; my peace I give to you. Not as the world gives do I give it to you. Do not let your hearts be troubled or afraid" (John14: 27). It was a message of consolation and hope for us. If we spend our time doing the work he gave us, guided and strengthened by the Holy Spirit, then we won't have time to cause unrest. Peace starts with the little things we do, and God will make their effects grow. Jesus said the world would hate us for it, but we should remember that he chose us, so we could leave the world behind us and keep our eyes focused on him (John 15:18–19). For the world to be at peace is most likely something only God can bring about. Peace for us comes when we busy ourselves doing God's will and learning to love him. Blessed Mother Teresa said, "We can only find true happiness and peace when we are in love with God: there is joy in loving God, great happiness in loving Him" (Teresa 1996, 84). Can we challenge ourselves this holiday season to discover the baby Jesus? Will we let his peace invade our hearts?

A WHISPERING VOICE

The jostling crowds of people were gone. They had come, almost in droves at first, to see the baby. The shepherds told everyone about the angel's message, and word spread quickly about a humble couple in a stable with a baby. Thank heavens God had directed them to on out-of-the-way cave to accommodate for the multitudes. Eventually though a kind-hearted family had taken them in as the census continued, for which Mary and Joseph were grateful. Now it was quieter, although guests still came most every day. Now a routine was developing with time for prayer.

What became Christmas is a busy time for us as well. And what a season it is: lights, music, gifts, family, food, and more, all to celebrate the birth of a small baby. In all the hoopla, it's a wonder Jesus doesn't get lost. Or does he? The Christmas season is loud with all the commotion surrounding it and our Lord is a simple, quiet voice. How often did we attend Mass with Christmas songs running through our minds or a movie segment for a rosary decade? It's not that Jesus doesn't want us to celebrate, for heaven's sake on his of all birthdays we should make merry, but he will not impose his voice unless we want to hear it. So how do we listen for God in a season that shouts of his birth? Ah, that's the catch! It will cost us something, but then anything worth having is worth paying for. Let's take a simple example from the Bible. In 1 Kings 19:9–13, the prophet Elijah goes into the wilderness to Mount Horeb and spends the night in a small cave. All these noisy things pass by: earthquakes, windstorms, and fires; but it was only in the gentle breeze that Elijah heard the voice of God. In essence, this is the same thing we must do. We don't have the luxury of going into a wilderness, so this is where silence will cost us. We need to turn off some aspects of the season to find minutes alone. Turn off the music or the movies; find some quiet time away from the crowds. Within our minds create our own quiet place, a calm in the midst of a storm. Jesus will be in the stillness. This is the birthplace of prayer. Unfortunately, this calm isn't achieved with only five minutes of silence. We must practice often until God isn't competing with the advertisements running through our heads. At times the silence comes easily; at others, it's a constant struggle (Jesus appreciates the struggle too.). In this silence, we find the presence of Jesus. He is a still, small voice whispering love songs to our hearts, and his heart will beat in unison with ours. This is the beginning: a spiritual glance, a sigh, an upward longing of our hearts to be with him—prayer. It is so simple and yet so difficult in this noisy world. If we want to be with him, we must make room for him. Every once in a while, let's take a few minutes to quiet ourselves and listen for the still, small voice of Jesus, a voice that will not shout to be heard but waits for us to turn our hearts willingly to him.

OUR NOISY HEARTS

Quite often when I find some peace and quiet and settle down, determined to get some good prayer time in, I ramble on with my own list of needs or complaints. I rattle them off then tell God what I think the best solution would be and ask what he's going to do about it, and then I'm done. What I haven't done is found the silence in my own heart, so I can hear what God has to say. I like what Bl. Mother Teresa of Calcutta said about prayer: "I always begin my prayer in silence, for it is in the silence of the heart that God speaks. God is the friend of silence - we need to listen to God because it's not what we say but what He says to us and through us that matters" (Teresa 1996, 5).

How often do we clutter up our prayer time with so many words? Yet that is what we learn especially in today's society. There seems to be a sense of "if there's silence, then something's wrong." Everywhere we go, there's music playing, TV blaring, cell phones ringing, etc. Communication is a great thing, and we are more connected now than ever before. But it seems that in all the clamor of communication, we do more speaking than we do listening. Somewhere the listening, or silent, end of communication got lost, almost to the point of our being uncomfortable when we find ourselves in it.

Even Jesus went off by himself to pray, away from the noisiness of people. In his prayer, he didn't try to impress God with poetic words but simply spoke from his heart. He spent time listening to what his Father had to say. Sometimes our prayer doesn't go that way. We may be so bound and determined to get a certain amount of prayers said in a day that we forget about God. Imagine if we were to come into our bedroom and, finding our spouse there, recite in all sincerity a beautiful poem about our love and life. Then as we finish and before the other can speak, we dash out of the room. It might leave the spouse wondering what just happened. Does this describe our relationship with God? Do we wake up in the morning, dash off our morning offering, and immediately start our day without giving God a chance to respond? Do we say the rosary with fervor and intense emotion, but was it good prayer? The same thing happens when we mumble our night prayers before tumbling into sleep. It's not prayer; it's a monologue. Is this the way two people in love should communicate? God doesn't want devotions that vary from day to day. He wants us.

The problem with silence is that it means allowing yourself not only to hear but also to listen to what someone says to you. Often, we aren't comfortable with such an intimate relationship—especially with God—because it may mean growth or change for us. We like our lives the way they are. Why mess with that? Because God knows us and only desires the best for our well-being. That's what love is. Our Father has so many love songs to sing for us if we would only let him.

So how do we learn this silence? In this case, the best way to learn is by doing. No need to start with hours-long meditations; start simply. Five minutes may be sufficient at first if we start growing restless. When we grow comfortable with that silence, we can find occasions of longer silence in our own prayers throughout the day. Soon we'll find ourselves listening for the gentle voice of our Lord and delighting in his words of love.

Let's try to take to heart Mother Teresa's advice and start our own prayers in silence. We never know how it will change us. The psalms themselves say, "I will listen for the word of God; surely the Lord will proclaim peace" (Ps. 85:9).

ORDINARY TIME I

The Presentation

Had it really been forty days since the birth of Jesus? Joseph counted again. Yes, the day was right. Time for him and Mary to take the baby to the temple where, according to the law of Moses, he would be presented to the Lord, and Mary would be purified after washing in the pool. Joseph considered their finances. Such an extended stay was draining their resources, and he knew they didn't have the five shekels required as ransom for the firstborn. Fortunately, carpentry was a skill needed everywhere, and Joseph was good at his craft. He managed to find enough work to put food on the table and a few necessities. Now, just outside the temple, he procured two pigeons, an acceptable ransom according to the law. He held them close and glanced over at Mary. She was holding Jesus just as tightly as they wove their way among the people. Her face radiated joy even through the sleepiness. The baby hadn't quite figured out yet the differences between night and day, and even now, moments before his presentation, he was sound asleep in his mother's arms. Joseph wished he were as calm. His heart beat hard against his chest as their turn approached. All the events surrounding Jesus's birth were so unusual, but the baby himself looks so normal. Would anything different be noticed? Would anyone know he wasn't the real father? Swallowing past the knot in his throat, Joseph handed over the pigeons, wishing desperately for actual silver, just in case. The priest held up the infant, intoned the prescribed prayers and handed the baby back to Joseph without another glance. It was done. Joseph released his breath. He hadn't realized he'd been holding it and smiled at Mary. Her eyes crinkled back at him. They started back toward the entrance but hadn't gone far when a figure approached. The man was so old and willowy, a good breeze would knock him over. His eyes though peered out of a leathery face with keen intensity, sweeping over the couple and settling on Jesus. Joseph thought he heard the man gasp, "The baby, my Lord?" as he bowed his head. Mary raised her eyebrows at Joseph, and Joseph shrugged, wondering at the fellow almost shaking before them. The old man opened his eyes and said, "I'm sorry. I've been waiting so long. My name is Simeon. May I?" he asked and held out his arms. Mary nodded consent, and Joseph handed over the baby to him. He was about to ask if he needed help but refrained when he felt Simeon's strong, wiry arms gently take the bundle. Simeon gazed into Jesus's face, his own face going through a mixture of emotions. Finally, with tears streaming down his cheeks, he raised the baby slightly and blessed God saying, "Now, Master, you can dismiss your servant in peace; you have fulfilled your word. For my eyes have witnessed your saving deed displayed for all the peoples to see: a revealing light to the Gentiles, and the glory of your people Israel" (Luke 2: 29–32).

He went on about the child being the rise and fall of many, then he pressed Jesus into Mary's arms, saying to her, "(And you yourself a sword will pierce) so that the thoughts of many hearts may be revealed" (Luke 2:33–35). The presence of the Lord was nearly palpable, and Mary bowed her head. She shivered at Simeon's words. Another elderly woman came and was speaking prophetically about Jesus. It was a lot to digest right then, and Mary just listened numbly, the words searing themselves into her heart. She gave them a tight-lipped smile as they turned to leave, and Joseph bade them go with God's blessings. Feeling Joseph put his arm around her shoulders, Mary sagged a little and hugged her baby to her chest. Joseph glanced around protectively and, seeing no one else across their path, quietly said to Mary, "Let's go," and they turned and left the temple.

Do I have to?

We all have tasks that we don't like doing. Some may dread meetings for work or speaking in front of people. Others may view class reunions as something to be gotten through. For me, I can't stand cleaning windows. Does that sound too cliché? We have old, wooden, drafty windows; they don't come out easily and need replacing badly. I let them go far too long in between washings. Windows are hardly the worst thing in anyone's life, but they'll make a good example. They're just one of those things that have to be done as a homeowner, so I take a deep breath and get out the squeegee. I know that even for something as silly as windows, I can go to God, and he'll give me the grace to smile as I clean. The point is that whatever the task or trial, if I go to God and ask his help, then he'll never let me go unprepared. He gives me all the grace I need. He does the same for any of us, just as he did for the holy family.

In Luke 2:22–35, we read about how Joseph and Mary took the baby Jesus to the temple for his presentation. Simeon came and praised Jesus, but he also gave a warning. Through Simeon, God told Mary that she would suffer as though she had been pierced by a sword. He was preparing her for what would lie ahead so that she wouldn't go into it blind. We don't know how much, if anything, Mary knew of Jesus's role beforehand, but we do know that she lived rooted in prayer. She pondered all the events of Jesus's life in her heart (Luke 2:51). Through Mary's going to God in prayer, he was able to give her the graces she would need to endure all. Mary had free will too, and she could have said no or that she would get through everything on her own, but she wisely chose to rely on God's strength. We can make the same choice.

Sometimes we forget how powerful having a free will can be. We can choose to say no. We can refuse to accept any help God might give us. So why are we forced to endure suffering and pain? Those things don't come from God, they are from the world. It's how we choose to endure them that's our purification, and if we ask his help, then we will triumph in the end. Even the sorrows of the world can be turned to good if it means coming closer to him.

As much as we might like for God to use skywriting or neon signs to communicate, usually we have to look to the people around us. Perhaps a quiet whispered word from a friend, a support or prayer group from church, any of these and more may be the help we need. God will speak to us in quiet ways and will always give the support necessary. We only have to recognize it when it comes, as Mary had to recognize the prophecy Simeon gave. Then armed with the strength that only God can give, we can withstand whatever the world may send.

EXILE

A nightmare, that's what this trip was. Joseph stopped to help Mary hoist herself up on the donkey again and handed her Jesus. Stars were starting to fade from the sky. Dawn would stop their journey for the day, and they'd find some out-of-the-way shelter to bed down. Traveling by daylight was too dangerous, especially after the rumors they heard about Bethlehem. Bethlehem. It seemed so long ago. A startling group had visited them—magi, or astrologers from foreign lands. They said they followed the star Joseph had seen shining over the city. Since they were apparently coming to see a new-born king, they proceeded to the palace. Herod knew nothing of it and was suspicious of their intent. He told the magi to report back to him when they found the baby. When they found Mary and Joseph, these grown men actually fell on their faces before Jesus! Gold, frankincense, and myrrh—so unusual—were given as gifts. Joseph wondered again who this baby would be. The magi stayed for some days and were about to head off to Herod but were warned against it in a dream. Instead, they returned to their own countries immediately. Joseph was also given a dream and told to take the baby and his mother into Egypt because Herod wanted Jesus dead. Such a message scared Joseph. Mary must have seen it in his eyes because she didn't say a word when he woke her and just started quickly gathering things. Joseph was relieved since he didn't know how he would explain to Mary if she'd protested. At first they'd traveled by day. Then once when stopping for supplies, Joseph heard a rumor that Herod had ordered all the baby boys up to age two killed in Bethlehem. When he told Mary, they held each other and wept for those children. From then on, they traveled as quickly as possible. The journey wasn't easy. Nights were cold, and they were rationing food to minimize stopping. What they would find in Egypt was a mystery to them. Maybe some Jewish communities were there so they hoped language wouldn't be too much of a problem. Joseph was good at his trade and fairly confident he could find some carpentry work. As long as they stayed inconspicuous and away from Herod's men, then maybe they could live in peace. His heart ached though. How would they live in a foreign land unable to worship in Jerusalem? What would it be like to raise a family among strangers? Would they ever return?

THE LOVE OF A CHILD

"Up! Mommy, I need up!" "I want to do it all by me self!" "Mommy, fix this!"—such were the demands I heard daily from my two-year-old daughter. Though the terrible twos are quite appropriately named, the title does leave out the gentler side: "I wuve you, Mommy." I thought infancy taught me about their dependence, but nothing prepared me for the love a child would learn to communicate in return. So often I wonder about Jesus at this age. What were the terrible twos like for Mary and Joseph? Aside from knowing they were raising the Son of God, did just the responsibilities of being parents overwhelm them? What did Mary think as she dressed a squirming toddler every day? Not only is this the age where children discover their independence, but equally important is what they come to understand about parents. In their little minds, Mommy and Daddy can do anything. Isn't that an awesome thought? Not only do we supply basic needs like feeding and clothing them, but we do the other thousand things like replacing batteries, tying shoes, and kissing boo-boos. Suddenly, I have this little girl climbing onto my lap and flinging her arms around my neck and whispering, "Mommy!" The amount of trust she places in me, and the love she has for me is overwhelming. Is this what Jesus meant when he said that we must be like children and accept the kingdom of heaven as a child does? (Mark 10:13–15). Can we honestly say that we love our Father as much as our children love us? Or perhaps our attitudes resemble more that of the terrible-twos child: "No! I want to do it all by me self!" How often do we test his patience and wander beyond the boundaries? How willingly do we accept our discipline? Do we ever give God the occasion to be overwhelmed by our trust in him?

Yet for all this, our God, in his unfailing wisdom and power, chose to become human like us. It seems we have a tough time loving him like a child so he had to show us how. He put his entire well-being into the care of his fallible creatures. He allowed himself to have parents who fed, bathed, and held him. He had someone who loved him and hugged him when he cried, and someone whom he could fling his arms around and whisper, "Mommy!" Do we have it in us to really believe that he knows what's best for us? Can we let go of our preconceptions of what we want in our lives and let him make the decisions? My daughter looks me in the eyes and knows that nothing else in the world matters as long as Mommy holds her. Do we dare to have the courage to trust our Father like a child, and to love him like a child, overwhelmingly?

INVISIBLE FRIENDS

How would I tell a child to come to Jesus? What would a child understand with only a child's capacities? One of a child's greatest assets is her imagination, so I would say to imagine Jesus much as she would an imaginary friend. Imagine him walking with her throughout her day, doing whatever it is she's doing, talk to him as she would a friend. Imagine his responses. In a child's mind, the child knows the imaginary friend knows her better than anyone else, so there is honesty in her thinking. If situations come up where a decision between right and wrong is necessary, perhaps this will be her conscience (a.k.a the Holy Spirit) speaking to her. If a child imagines Jesus and not just any person, she can consider what God is thinking about what she's doing and then (hopefully) be more likely to make the right decision. It's the beginning of always considering what Jesus would do and whether her actions please him. Does is seem like play? Does it seem too silly? But Jesus said unless we become like children. That doesn't mean to be childish in our thoughts and actions but to have the innocence and unconditional love and trust of children. Is it too much for us to imagine Jesus this way, like an imaginary friend? Consider it a challenge because this is prayer. It won't be some deep, profound experience, but it is a beginning, a turning of our thoughts to him. That's all prayer is really. Perhaps, at first, this kind of prayer will be more relevant to us rather than trying to sit still and think about some mystical person out there somewhere. God doesn't want to be out there somewhere. He wants to be right here, living our life with us, walking with us step by insignificant step. Not every minute of our lives is some glorious offering to God; more often, our lives are quiet, routine moments. He wants in there too. When we take those quiet moments and just live them with God walking with us, much like an imaginary friend, then we've united those moments to him, and it has become prayer. Is something so simple still considered prayer? Yes. Because as Jesus walks with us throughout our day, we start to think differently. And rather than *I* need to do such and such, we think *we* need to do this. Our day becomes filled with "he and I." This way, we're always living in his presence. We don't have to talk all the time. Sometimes he's just there with us. And if we discover we've done something without thinking of him, then just imagine him again right where you are. He's happy every time we think of him. It's a beginning. Take the challenge.

LOST

The temple was buzzing with all the pilgrims there for the Passover as twelve-year-old Jesus wound his way among them. His parents were getting ready to leave, and he'd gone back and forth between the men's and women's caravans, trying to help but was laughingly shooed away each time. The festive days had been filled with large gatherings of relatives not seen in ages and all-encompassing hugs and kisses. Food and prayer wove together the preparations for Passover, and the days were busy. Now they were bustling about, trading last stories and goods as they loaded the animals. To stay out from under-foot, Jesus thought he'd go to the temple one last time. The temple of Jerusalem, the heart of Jewish worship, was amazing. His family had come every year since they'd returned from Egypt so long ago, and he never tired of gazing at the gold and marble stonework, smelling the incense, and hearing the Levites' songs. Even though the eight days of the Pesach were laced with ritual prayer, some quiet prayer time now would be enjoyable. Finding a place behind a pillar, the boy leaned against a wall and closed his eyes, letting his spirit drift with the echoing psalms being chanted.

Joseph and Mary were frantic. For three days, they'd scoured the city, searching among nearly a million people, but no one had seen their son. How had this happened? They'd been such diligent parents. Now the temple, still crowded, loomed over them as they drew near. The two crossed the Temple Mount in several places, looking through various porticos until suddenly Joseph gripped Mary's hand. "Over there." Mary stood on tiptoe but couldn't see over the heads. Joseph pulled her through a gathering of people who were listening to some rabbi, and then she heard Jesus's voice. What? These people were all focused on Jesus? She took a deep breath and held back a sob. He was okay. She let loose of Joseph's hand and flew to her son, gathering him in a quick embrace. She knew he was considered a man now at twelve, but he was still her son, missing for three days and she would hug him. She stepped back and felt her husband come up from behind. "Son," she said as she grabbed his hand in both of hers "why have you done this to us? Your father and I have been looking for you with great anxiety." And he said to them, "Why were you looking for me? Did you not know I must be in my Father's house?" (Luke 2:49).

TAKE CARE OF EACH OTHER

You know how some things just smack you between the eyes and make you think, Hey, wake up and smell the coffee! I had one of those instances just after New Year. I honestly don't even remember the specific infraction that occurred, only that one of my daughters and her friend were doing something they shouldn't have been. My daughter knew the rules and failed to tell her friend, so when I got the story straight and they told me what had happened, I was more furious with my girl than I was with the other one because she knew my expectations. Needless to say, my daughter's punishment was a little stiffer. The comparison of what happened didn't strike me until later:

"If I tell the wicked man that he shall surely die, and you do not speak out to dissuade the wicked man from his way, he (the wicked man) shall die for his guilt, but I will hold you responsible for his death. But if you warn the wicked man, trying to turn him from his way, and he refuses to turn from his way, he shall die for his guilt, but you shall save yourself" (Ezek. 33:8–9).

Ouch. That's tough. Let that sink in for a moment. So even though we know the rules and we act according to them, thinking we are saving ourselves, but if we, in our apathy, let others do their own thing because, hey, it's their life, we are dooming ourselves because God will say to us, "You knew better than that. If they didn't know the right thing, then tell them!" At the end of our lives, we can't smugly look around and say, "Well, I lived a good life by what Jesus said so I should be fine." No, because if we let our friends (or others) go blindly on their way when we know it's wrong but we don't want to step on toes, then God will hold us responsible.

So does this mean we adopt a holier-than-thou attitude? Absolutely not! We cannot say that we are better than someone else because we do this or that or start condemning people. Bullhorns aren't necessarily the best approach. Look at each situation individually, use the practical wisdom we've been given, and use tact. Prayerfully discern the best way to make God's will known and then stand back. Much as we might like to save everyone, we can't force it. Not even God does that. We must always be smaller and realize that God's way is the best way, and even we are still learning his way while we teach others.

Sometimes I am awed by the responsibility of being a Christian, yet we mustn't shrink. If we cling to the hem of God's mercy and follow where he leads, we can joyfully trust he won't lead us astray. Whether we're teaching our children, standing up for our moral rights, or simply being a good example for our neighbors, we can let his light shine out in us. Our God is good, and he holds us all in the palm of his hand. Blessed be God forever.

I WANT TO BE A STAR

The Bible is silent about the early years of Jesus. Except for one brief passage about him getting lost in the temple, there is nothing. After all the excitement of angels, dreams, and exile, we might think the extraordinary continued. More likely, since there is nothing recorded, only normal stuff happened. Perhaps it's not as much fun to write about, or maybe the gospel authors thought no one would read the ordinary. Honestly, even today, the media is filled with the attention-getting headlines, and when we read about heroic deeds, do we wonder, "Wow, could I do that? Could I make such a sacrifice?" Perhaps we like having our pictures splashed across social media. Maybe it takes us out of the humdrum of normal life and makes our stories known. We tend to love the excitement of doing the big things; we relish the extraordinary. But what happens when God calls us to love the ordinary? Are we satisfied with that? Do we still believe we are accomplishing anything for him? Which takes the larger effort, the ordinary or the extraordinary?

As a culture in general, we tend to seek out the extreme or anything that will bring us attention. Sometimes it's fun being in the spotlight, other times not, but it's still attention. We're noticed. Realistically, those moments are few. For the most part, we're called to live quietly in obedience to what God places before us at the moment. How well are we doing that? I ask myself, "If God asks me to pray every day, do I?" I may start out well, but do I get bored and become sporadic? How hard is that obedience then! But isn't it that way with everything? When we're driving through town, we obey the traffic signals. If we disobey, we get pulled over. Isn't it funny, that when we do what we're supposed to, nobody notices? That's hard for us. Yet it's only when we're obedient to God that we really accomplish what he asks, no matter how big or small it seems to us. We don't see the other side of the picture from here. Perhaps our daily prayers are needed for the conversion of a soul half a continent away. We may never know. All we can do is be faithful to what he asks. Like any parent, God will only ask us small things at first, things we can handle, like praying or cleaning or any mundane routine in our lives. If we do these things well, perhaps he will ask of us something larger a time or two.

A prime example of someone who was obedient her whole life is Mary, mother of Jesus. At times, her life may have seemed exciting, what with angelic messages and God being her son and all, but how many days of her life do we really know about? Mostly, she lived quietly in Nazareth with Joseph and Jesus, working, praying, and doing her daily duty. It was for that perfect obedience, which her neighbors never noticed, that we know her now.

Ask ourselves again: If Mary asks us to pray, pray, and pray more every day, are we obeying even that smallest of requests? If God were to ask that we live our lives joyfully, offering him even our most mundane work that we tire of, could we make that sacrifice and obey?

Jesus's ministry

I will be with you always...even in ordinary time. Okay, so that's not quite how Jesus said it, but it's pretty close. January and February mark the beginning of Ordinary Time, the largest season of the church calendar. Why, when there are so many things to celebrate, devote so much time to ordinariness? In the gospels, nothing of what happens can really be deemed ordinary, that's why those events were written down. Only the extraordinary makes the news. The simplest thing Jesus did during his ministry years was to use a common method—parables—to teach the people. In the fifth through seventh chapters of Matthew, Jesus essentially tells us how to live in a manner pleasing to the Father in the common things of life. Don't be conspicuous when we fast, for example, but act normally. Our Father knows what we are doing and accepts our actions in the quietness of our hearts. It's the everyday occurrences we must rely on to make our daily sacrifice. If we offered only the extraordinary, most of us wouldn't have much to offer. Even St. Therese of Lisieux knew the value of the littlest things as she was continually offering up the monotony of each day to God. Sometimes such offerings are the harder of the two to accomplish. Still we have to learn to be trustworthy and reliable in the little things; otherwise, how will he trust us in the larger?

On my little altar, I have a statue of Mary holding up the baby Jesus airplane-style, above her head and looking into his face, much the way any mother holds up her baby in joy. He experienced every aspect of life just as we do. He's always been there for us, never changing, throughout our entire lives. He's known every little joy and sorrow we've known and has gathered into his heart all our tiniest offerings. It's awesome to think that someone can be so faithful that they're with us every minute of our lives and still love us!

In the gospels, we're shown that Jesus knows how hard it is to be loving and faithful without a little lift now and then. In Matthew, chapter 17, Jesus took Peter, James, and John up onto a mountain where they saw him transfigured. We can guess that it was a very uplifting and intense moment for all of them, perhaps one of those high moments where they uniquely experienced the splendor of God. If we listen to the spirit in our lives, then we know that Jesus also gives us such moments when we can feel God's love overwhelmingly. Often the memory of those moments gives us the strength to endure the daily routine till the next grace. Even Jesus had to come down from the mountain and face the ordinariness of life, but he does give us graces to help along the way.

So perhaps Ordinary Time is an unwitting reflection of our own lives: mostly commonplace with highlights here and there. Jesus is still there, walking right along with us, loving us through everything. Now we must ask how well do we, how eager are we, to love him in the monotony of each day?

But I had plans

Every once in a while I am glaringly reminded of my own lack of trust in God. It's not distrust; it's just a realization that I could trust him far more than I do. I had a set of plans made up for the day (one of those rare free days when the girls are at a sitter) of things to accomplish and then simply relaxing for a bit. However, just after I dropped off the girls, circumstances changed and I ended up not doing a thing I had planned but dealing with car troubles the rest of the day. I was not happy. I actually argued with God about it for a bit, saying that I knew this was where he must have wanted me at the moment, but it's *not* where *I* wanted to be. I finally let him take over, and I managed to not get into arguments etc., and resolved the day fairly peacefully.

So what did I learn from all this, and how? Mary helped. She and Joseph probably hadn't intended to have Jesus in a cave. They hadn't planned on exile in Egypt or losing Jesus in Jerusalem or any other number of incidents. The couple in Cana hadn't planned to run out of wine at their wedding. Things happen, and I can't rely on myself to fix the problem with the finesse that God could fix it. Mary knows that God can do anything, so she simply tells us, "Do whatever he tells you" (John 2:5), even when what he says is a bit beyond the rational realm. (What good is it going to do to fill those jars with water? I need wine here. Jesus, really.) Jesus changed water into wine! How fantastic is that? What about when the Israelites came up to Jericho? God told them to march around the city for seven days and then blow their horns and yell like crazy. No one in their right mind would believe that would defeat a city. Yet they trusted in God, so he fulfilled his word and the walls came down. The way God works is far stranger and more inventive than we could ever imagine. G. K. Chesterton once wrote, "Truth, of course, must of necessity be stranger than fiction, for we have made fiction to suit ourselves" (Chesterton, 1919). Jesus is the way, the truth, and the life (John 14:6). Anything we do apart from Jesus might as well be fiction. Admittedly, the examples above were larger-than-life, but we have to trust God completely in the little things before he can do the big things with us. ("So he was not able to perform any mighty deed there...He was amazed at their lack of faith" [Mark 6:5–6].) We need to trust daily his divine providence for every crumb of bread, not to mention everything else. Only in this way can we realize that when things don't go our way, maybe that's what God had in mind for our purification or for the furthering of his kingdom. We don't have to passively accept whatever comes our way, but perhaps we can try embracing it instead. Say rather, "Okay, this is my lot. What can I do with it? How can my reaction best be an example of Christ living in me?" And only through this can we reflect the truth of Jesus in us and finally live God's will, proclaiming him who is the way, the truth, and the life to all we meet.

OFFERING OUR BEST

"It's mine!" "No, it's mine!" "I had it first!" Then the wails started as my preschooler won out over my toddler. I've become an excellent referee in the past couple of years. More importantly, I've learned a lot of lessons about human behavior. I see how my girls make mistakes and how I deal with them, and I see how we adults make mistakes and how God must deal with us as his children. As I repeatedly tell my children to share and play nice, I am reminded of how often God tells us those very things. "From the person who takes your cloak, do not withhold even your tunic" (Luke 6:29). "Lend expecting nothing back" (Luke 6: 35). The gospels are full of Jesus telling us to love others and be generous. Apparently, it goes against our fallen human nature to be generous. So like we do to our children, Jesus must remind us over and over again to share. How pleased he must be when we finally listen! Jesus was just watching the rich people tossing their offerings into the box, but when a poor widow offered two pennies, he rejoiced! Here at last was someone who offered God what was from their means of life, the best they could offer, and who didn't give God just the leftovers. How often is that our attitude though, that we'll just give what we have to? I don't mean just with money, but with things and time as well. I know I do it all the time with my children. "Girls, let me finish what I'm doing, then I'll come help." Or if I'm eating something I really enjoy, I'll try to hide it from them so I don't have to share as much. (Yes, I need to learn my own lessons!) Yet I know God wants me to be so much more generous than that. In chapter 4 of Genesis, Cain brought to God an offering from his harvest of crops. Abel, however, brought God one of the best firstlings of his flock. God was pleased with Abel's offering; it was from the best he had. If we're going to offer something to God or to each other, shouldn't it be the best we have or the best we can do? Doesn't it seem that halfhearted offerings are almost more of an insult? We'd be saying, I'm giving or doing this only because I have to. Even King David said, "I cannot offer to the Lord my God holocausts that cost nothing" (2 Sam. 24:24). Our offerings don't have to be huge and elaborate. They're whatever we're capable of. Sometimes the best offering is something we don't want to do, but for his sake, we willingly do it anyway. How often Jesus said, "I desire mercy, not sacrifice" (Matt. 12:7). If we stop to give him our best, then he will reward us a hundredfold. Isn't that worth the effort?

COME WITH ME

I admit I've done the out-of-breath rosary routine. I try to wake up earlier than my girls just to find some quiet, but I won't have gotten up early enough and end up cutting myself short. For the next few minutes, I'm out of sorts. I didn't get to ask God what he desires for me, and I didn't give him time to whisper a reply. (Maybe it was his will that I be disturbed. My own grumbling tells me that I have yet to learn to submit myself entirely to his will in every situation.) But this is where living in God's presence becomes necessary. I then continue my conversation with him as I fix my girls their breakfast. I ask for help, controlling my patience when I wipe up the third cup of spilled milk. I talk to my Father in each event that occurs, thereby, praising, interceding, thanking, etc. Even in extreme circumstances, sometimes especially in them, I know that God is there with me. I imagine that Jesus is at my side, observing, simply letting his presence be felt. Words aren't necessary all the time. Instead, there is the beating of two hearts.

Perhaps the next time we feel inclined to rush off after our prayers, we can take God with us instead of leaving him behind. Our prayers and pious acts aren't ends in themselves. God himself is our focus. Be so aware of his presence that we see him in every person and situation. Nothing can distract us then. We can start by simply asking, "Jesus, come walk with me."

WHAT REALLY MATTERS

There are some days when life goes really fast. Between working, grocery shopping, fixing meals, homework, getting kids bathed, etc., I sit down and find that my feet hurt up almost up to my knees (probably because of a bad choice in shoes). A rather ordinary day, or what I call a peanut-butter-and-jelly day. Not every meal is going to be gourmet cuisine, and not every day is going to stand out. You have to have the regular food that keeps you going in between the spectacular. So as I look back on my peanut-butter-and-jelly day, I wonder if I got caught up in business or if I did anything that really mattered.

During the three years of Jesus's public ministry, I'm sure that Jesus must have had some of those same days. Were the people catching on to his message? At the end of the day, did he feel like anything he did made a difference? I can't imagine how hectic Jesus's day was with all the thousands of people coming to him. With everyone wanting him, pulling his attention this way and that, keeping focus might have been pretty hard.

When we cram a myriad of things into one day, sometimes we can discover what our priorities actually are by looking at our schedule. We might like to think some things are high priority but our actions will speak clearly to us. We'll make the time to do what we feel is most important. If we say, "God is number one in my life," then we should see evidence of that in our day. Do we take time to pray every day and let our lives revolve around that relationship? Or do we instead find our days filled with appointments and media and distractions? I recently spent a weekend with some people who, when they woke up, hit the floor running and kept that pace the entire day with no time for prayer. Even in their downtime, prayer didn't enter the picture. I found it very disquieting. I love my Lord. I need to run to him often and tell him so. Apparently, Jesus felt the same need since he was often going off by himself and escaping the crowds. "Then Jesus was led by the Spirit into the desert" (Matt. 4:1); "He withdrew in a boat to a deserted place by himself" (Matt. 14:13); "He went off to the mountain to pray" (Mark. 6:46); "He would withdraw to deserted places to pray" (Luke 5:16); "In those days he departed to the mountain to pray, and he spent the night in prayer to God" (Luke6:12). The gospels are filled with such examples. If Jesus wasn't too busy to pray, then I also need to find the balance between work and prayer. Balance also helps keep priorities straight in dealing with people. Therefore, consider whether or not we're too busy to be civil with the people we deal with in our day or to tell even the people around us that we love them. What if it's the last time we see that person? (It happens all too often.) Were we kind to them? Did we leave them better off for having met us, and did we help them on their journey? Did we tell them we love them, using just those words? If we were to die today, what regrets would we have? When we come to stand before God, he isn't going to ask us how much we did or how much of a theologian we were, he's going to ask us how much we loved.

So that's it, plain and simple. Did we love each other? Did we tell God that we loved him? I apologized to my girls for my foul temper today, and we all prayed for each other. I gave my family hugs and said "I love you" to each one before bed. If nothing else, I told my family that they really mattered to me. Praised be Jesus, now and forever.

WE HAVE TO DO WHAT?

Jesus raised his voice over the murmuring and tried explaining it again. As he spoke, his voice took on majesty, and he felt the Holy Spirit filling him, adding emphasis to his words,

> "I say to you, unless you eat the flesh of the Son of Man and drink his blood, you do not have life within you. Whoever eats my flesh and drinks my blood has eternal life, and I will raise him on the last day. For my flesh is true food, and my blood is true drink. Whoever eats my flesh and drinks my blood remains in me and I in him. Just as the living Father sent me and I have life because of the Father, so also the one who feeds on me will have life because of me. This is the bread that came down from heaven. Unlike your ancestors who ate and still died, whoever eats this bread will live forever." (John 6:53–58)

The silence was deafening. Then the crowd erupted. For the Jewish people, it was scandalous. How could Jesus be the bread that came down from heaven? Surely, no manna had come since Moses's time, and Jesus was a flesh-and-blood human being. What did he mean, people should eat his flesh? Honestly! Jesus looked at his apostles. They whispered among themselves, trying to digest this bit of information. Did they yet understand his mission, the sacrifice he would make to give them and everyone life? Did they know that he would never leave them, even if the world would have them believe otherwise? "Do you also want to leave?" Simon Peter answered him, "Master, to whom shall we go? You have the words of eternal life" (John 6:68). Jesus's heart leapt for joy.

ONE MAN'S COURAGE

"Take courage and be a man. Keep the mandate of the Lord, your God, following his ways and observing his statutes, commands, ordinances and decrees… that you may succeed in whatever you do"

(1 Kings 2:2–3)

What an example we've been given to follow in John Paul II! Consider all the things people said about the late pope and how courageous/ hard-necked he was about applying the church's teachings. Such characteristics are noteworthy to applaud, and we feel good doing so, but how much will we really let his courage penetrate our heart? I pray that we let his inspiration take hold of us and enable us to stand firm against all the errors of the world.

There are some who would like to pick and choose which doctrines they believe in, but we can't be cafeteria catholics. If we profess to belonging to the Catholic Church then we must accept what she teaches. Church teaching isn't subject to democratic scrutiny. Consider this: When Moses came down from Mt. Sinai with God's invitation to covenant, the people said yes, they would do all that the Lord said. Moses went back up on the mountain to hammer out the details. Meanwhile, the people became restless and started worshipping a golden bull. Now when Moses came back down from Mt. Sinai, a majority of the people were worshipping the Apis bull cult (after they'd said yes to God), so does that mean the Ten Commandments dictated by God were not an authentic teaching? I hope we can keep our eyes focused on the truth and not be swayed by false or otherwise appealing ideas.

St. John Paul II was for us a beacon of light in a world running rampant in error. He had the courage to voice God's teachings even when the popular opinion ran the other way. He didn't back down in the face of opposition as we so often do when we know we're up against the odds. How often do we compromise when we're afraid of what other people might think? Why is it that we so often allow ourselves to base our lives on other people's respect when people today don't respect God? Is it simply fear? John Paul, echoing Jesus Christ, said, "Do not be afraid." Jesus himself reassured us when he said that we would suffer in the world. He said, "Take courage, I have conquered the world" (John 16:33). And Jesus can do anything.

How's our vision?

> "It is only with the heart that one can see rightly;
> what is essential is invisible to the eye"

> (de Saint-Exupery 1943, 70)

Look around the room and see everything that's red. Didn't every red item suddenly seem to pop out at you? That's because you were focused on seeing something specific, and everything else faded into the background. The test was simply a practical application of something we do in our lives. How do we see events and people around us? What filters do we see through? If we look at things with a critical eye and focus only on gossip and scandal, that's exactly what we'll find. Or do we instead try to find the positive and the good that people do? It's said that 10 percent of life is action and 90 percent reaction. Our reactions depend on how we choose to view things and our attitude. Society today has fostered a competitive attitude so that we look with a critical and judgmental eye. We place ourselves on a higher level than others: I'm better at this, my clothes are nicer; I know more than they do; etc. It's easy to do this because it's what we're used to doing. How much more difficult to see others (and ourselves) through God's eyes? How do we know how God sees?

"Do nothing out of selfishness or out of vainglory; rather, humbly regard others as more important than yourselves, each looking out not for his own interests, but [also] everyone for those of others. Have among yourselves the same attitude that is also yours in Christ Jesus" (Phil. 2:3–5).

In all humility, Jesus chose to be born human even though he was God. So once he was here, did he condemn us? In chapter 10 of Mark, verse 21, concerning Jesus's reaction to the rich man, it says, "Jesus, looking at him, loved him." So much in so few words! Jesus looked beyond the rich man with all his trappings and saw just the man his Father had created. He saw a soul for what it was, faults and all, and saw a soul to be loved. Can we do that? Not on our own. Only by God's grace through prayer do we have the strength to love and see things as Jesus does. Blessed Mother Teresa says, "Prayer feeds the soul—as blood is to the body, prayer is to the soul—and it brings you closer to God. It also gives you a clean and pure heart. A clean heart can see God, can speak to God, and can see the love of God in others" (Mother Teresa 1996, 5).

Can we build up and not tear down the community of Christ? Is the cost too much to look with the eyes of love, with the eyes of Jesus? Do we dare?

FRIENDS FOREVER

"I no longer call you slaves…I have called you friends" (John 15:15). And to think that Jesus directed those words to us! But what does it mean to be a friend?

Friendship was obviously something important to Jesus. He was closer to some apostles than others (Peter, James, and John), and he wept when his friend Lazarus died. If Jesus considered friends important, then perhaps we should take a closer look at our friendships as well. "A faithful friend is a life-saving remedy, such as he who fears God finds; For he who fears God behaves accordingly, and his friend will be like himself" (Sir. 6:16–17). It's a rough world out there, and Jesus knows that. He told us that because he'd chosen us out of the world, the world would hate us but that it also hated him first (John 15:18 19). When he sent out the disciples, he sent them two by two (Mark 6:7), so they could support each other in love of God and neighbor. We are still today like sheep among wolves, and when the wolves get us down or we feel like we've been battered by the storms, we need friends there to be strong when we are weak. This is why it's so important to choose friends wisely. Chapters 6 and 13 of Sirach continue to say to test our friends—do they drag us down or lift us up? Do we pick up their bad habits (and they ours) or do we help each other on the journey to God? But evaluating our friendships doesn't mean we immediately abandon those that aren't godly. Can we be a witness of Jesus's love and light? Some friendships must be kept like family, neighbors, and coworkers; and perhaps, those are more trying. Maybe the difficult relationships are a test for us in charity and a chance to see our own weaknesses. We all have our faults. God the Father told St. Catherine of Siena, "This is why I have put you among your neighbors: so that you can do for them what you cannot do for me- that is, love them without any concern for thanks and without looking for any profit for yourself. And whatever you do for them I will consider done for me" (St. Catherine of Siena 1995).

This is one way we grow in holiness: dealing well with others.

As we consider and thank God for our friends, let's not forget to evaluate ourselves and how good of a friend we are. Do we also affect others for the better? If we find ourselves lacking, pray and God will help us. That's what friends are for.

LENT

Determination

Jesus leaned against the rock after his early morning climb up the mountain. With the sun still below the horizon, the world had a rather blue-gray tint. He breathed in the silence, relishing the quiet away from the hunger of the people. The crowds kept growing despite the fair number of enemies he was making. He was anxious though about his apostles. Twice already he'd warned them about his coming passion, but they'd just given him puzzled looks. Passover was in a few weeks. He'd try again. He knew they wouldn't really understand until after, but he wanted them a little prepared if only to lessen the shock. He remembered his teaching them about the shepherd and his sheep. Did they understand yet that the shepherd would be devoured by the wolves for a time? The thought of what he was to undergo and his love for his flock made his heart constrict. Crying out to his Father in heaven, Jesus fell to his knees, bending low, his face almost touching the ground. Father, he prayed, use me to show the world how much we love them. Show your children your passion for them.

Jesus thought back to creation. After the physical world was made, his Father said, "Let us make man in our image, after our likeness" (Gen. 1:26). So human beings' physical body and immortal soul were created. Then we breathed life into their form. We breathed in our love, thoughts, longings, desires, and our reasoning. So great was our love that, like any parent, it took form outside our being so our children could freely love us in return. An aching filled Jesus's heart as he remembered how the design of walking in the Garden of Eden with their creation was shattered by the devil. Such a fall, to choose darkness over the light! The sorrow of their banishment still seared his being, but their pain prevented them from staying in God's direct presence any longer; our light burned the darkness that'd filled them.

Humans had to repent from that choice. We had so wanted them to be with us forever, and now the only option is a very straight and narrow path back to heaven. We would do anything to keep them from going astray; oh, how to make them understand?

He remembered the unspoken agreement among them, the sacrifice they would make. There was never any question, any doubt. Even now with Passover just weeks away, he hasn't regretted any of it. Jesus smiled inwardly at the thought of his mother's creation. She was so beautiful. She hadn't turned away; she'd chosen God every step of her life. What joy to become human as her child, to be nestled in her arms and guided by one who so closely resembled the Father. Ah, Mother! What she was about to endure for him. He so wanted to shield her from this, but Mary too had a road to travel. Already she understood that the Father used any suffering joined with Jesus's own for a greater purpose, one that she may not completely understand in this life.

Becoming human had been the best way to reach their children, living a life of hardship and toil with them, living in a way they could understand. Here he'd been able to preach to their brokenness, demonstrating God's love, mercy, and forgiveness through his own actions. Would they remember that there's more to this life than what they see? Could they keep they focus on heaven, their home, and not be distracted on the journey? Being their teacher and guide wasn't enough. Roaming preachers abounded with good messages, but people still forgot them after a while. Not only did they need to remember, a more powerful battle needed to be won, the one that had closed the gates of heaven. He needed to become their suffering servant in every way to break the bond that Satan had over them and open the gates. He knew the passion he'd endure. It'd been foretold in the scriptures: "So marred was his look beyond that of man, and his appearance beyond that of mortals" (Isa. 52:14). He would die. Jesus shuddered. Even though he was God, he still had a human heart and feelings and couldn't help feeling a certain terror at the thought. He could do it. He'd do it for them to bring them back. He had to show them how much they were loved by the Father, by all of them. "That they may all may be one, as you, Father, are in me and I in you, that they also may be in us" (John 17:21). Help them, by my resurrection, to endure not only what the world throws at them but to live, strengthened by our love and truth, to fight against the darkness. I'll bring them home, Father. I'll bring them home. In the morning stillness, Jesus looked at the sun, well above the horizon now. He took a deep breath and headed down the mountain.

Lent, the six and a half weeks before Easter, is a time of intense preparation for the celebration of Jesus's death and resurrection. Forty days for Lent (not including Sundays) were chosen for a variety of reasons. Biblically, the number 40 represents "a long time." The Israelites spent forty years wandering in the desert after leaving Egypt. Jesus went into the desert for a forty-day fast before beginning his ministry. So too we take our souls on a journey into the desert, stripping ourselves bare of the nonessentials. We put a mirror before ourselves and look honestly and deeply, hearing again the question God asked to Adam, "Where are you?" Will we hide or will we try to answer truthfully, "Where are we?"

EXERCISING OUR SOULS

"What are you giving up for Lent?" is a popular question as Lent approaches. Giving up something has almost become a fad and not a spiritual exercise. Perhaps we ought to reexamine our motivations for sacrifice to make a more meaningful journey to Easter.

Saying, "I'm giving up chocolate" or "I'm giving up TV" is easy, but why give anything up at all? Are we actually giving something up only to replace it with more meaningless activity? Do we make the sacrifice for the sake of sacrificing without thought of the goal? This appeared to be a common problem even in Jesus's day. As an offering of petition or thanksgiving, a sacrifice of animals was offered, often with good intent but maybe sometimes without thought. Anyone could go to the temple, purchase an animal, and give it to the priest to sacrifice. But how often was that sacrifice thought to make things right or offer atonement without effort? Jesus frequently debated the Pharisees about these very matters, between the letter and the spirit of the law! Jesus's humanness comes through quite easily when we read that "he sighed from the depth of his spirit" (Mark 8:12). Perhaps this was why Jesus so often quoted Hosea 6:6: "I desire mercy, not sacrifice" (Matt. 9:13). He knew burnt offerings didn't do the job; effort is required on the part of the person. Which would be harder? To be kind and forgiving or to offer up a pigeon? It's far more beneficial to offer the kind word although there are times I'd rather offer the pigeon!

A wonderful quote to keep in mind is "I cannot offer to the Lord my God holocausts that cost nothing" (2 Sam. 24:24). Maybe the focus shouldn't be "giving up" but rather "giving in" to the spirit of God in us. So many times we don't have the courage to love when we ought, but courage comes from God. We just need to ask for it, as he can do things we can't. Asking comes in the form of prayer. Prayer doesn't necessarily change the things or people around us, but it will change us individually. It molds our hearts to be more like the heart of Jesus. Suddenly saying that kind word isn't so difficult—we want to. That, to God, may be a bigger offering than all the sweets put together.

Does this mean we shouldn't give up the extras this Lent? Not at all! Easter is the biggest feast of the church year and appropriate preparation is needed. We are celebrating the central act of salvation history: the death and resurrection of Jesus. Just as we get cleaned and dressed up for Easter Mass, our souls need to be purified too. With the right intentions, acts like giving up coffee or the radio say to God, "See, I love you so much I'm willing to go without these things and feed my soul instead." Replace the movie with a meditation on the passion of Jesus. Jesus's foretelling of his death and resurrection was another topic the disciples "did not understand" (Luke 9:45). Did Jesus ever wonder, dropping his head into his hands, what he was ever going to do to make us understand? Even though we have hindsight and say we understand his rising from the dead, do we really? Do we live like it has a meaning for us personally? For every urge for sweets, offer up a quick prayer for the souls in purgatory. Use every minute of Lent to surround ourselves with the life and death of Jesus so we can share in his resurrection. St. Paul says that an athlete preparing to run a race will deny himself (1 Cor. 9: 24–27). We do the same in preparing for Easter with a goal of having him alive in our hearts. Let's truly look at our motivations for sacrifice this Lent and make a good preparation. Try to end Lent with the sacrament of reconciliation to completely purify ourselves then rejoice and celebrate, for the Lord will be risen indeed!

HOUSE CLEANING

> "We have to try to give Jesus to our youth. They must be able to look up and see Jesus. And they must be able to see Him in the home"
>
> (Mother Teresa 1983, 61).

I made a mistake the other day. I was coming home with my preschool girls in the car, and I switched on the radio. In the one, maybe two minutes it was on before I hurriedly switched it back off, my girls heard a newscast about a woman who slit her baby's throat, using those words. Well, that was enough. Immediately after and since that day, I have fielded questions about why she did that. I'm not sure they realize the baby died—thank heavens—as they don't understand the vocabulary. Along with various discussions, I've made it an opportunity to pray with my girls for other people.

The whole episode made me think again of what we allow into our homes and how that affects what we think. Our Father wants us to be pure in body, heart, and mind. How saturated are we with images of violence, sexual impurity, drunkenness, obscene jokes, and the like? Do we even notice when we see these things or do we just brush them aside and say, "Oh, that's just the way things are"? Jesus calls us away from all that. We are supposed to set our thoughts on higher things, on heaven rather than earth. St. Paul says to direct our thoughts toward what is pure, decent, deserves respect, virtuous, and worthy of praise (Phil. 4:8). Especially during Lent, we are called to holiness. Our sacrifices are meant to strip us of some earthly pleasures so that we have more room for him in our lives. "As he who called you is holy, be holy yourselves in every aspect of your conduct, for it is written, 'Be holy because I [am] holy'" (1 Pet. 1:15–16). The Father calls us, as earthen vessels, to be temples worthy of his Holy Spirit. How are we to do that while living in a world seemingly ruled by the prince of darkness? "How can the young walk without fault?" (Ps. 119:9). Can we shut ourselves up in a cocoon? No, not really because Jesus instructed us to go out to all the world and preach the good news. So we are to get our hands dirty on the front lines of converting souls. That doesn't mean we can't make our homes a refuge. "I act with integrity of heart within my royal court. I do not allow into my presence anyone who speaks perversely" (Ps. 101:2–3). Our homes need to be for us a place of refreshment, and if necessary, a refuge to escape the rigors of the world and be strengthened. It is our responsibility to set a good example for our families by watching the content of what enters our homes. Are these books, magazines, or movies, something we would read/watch if Jesus were beside us? Do we have prayer time for our children to imitate? Are we embarrassed to hang a picture of Jesus on the wall? Children will follow our example. While we are purifying our souls this Lent, perhaps we should purify our homes as well. Then our Father in heaven can look on our families and smile since he sees something beautiful for him.

Bare bones

The bareness of Lent struck me early on this year when I was late taking down the Christmas decorations. I like all the decorations, songs, lights, smells, and hoopla. They help put us in the Christmas spirit. The same concept goes for our spiritual life. If we perform acts of piety (with honest intent), then hopefully, they will eventually make us more pious and vice versa. There are all sorts of novenas and particular devotions we can follow. Now while it's all nice and enhances our life as Catholics, is it required? If we strip away, like the Christmas decorations, all the ornamentation, all the piety, and all the devotions, we will be left with the bare essence of what it means to be Christian: "You have been told, O man, what is good, and what the Lord requires of you: Only to do the right and to love goodness, and to walk humbly with your God" (Mic. 6:8).

Which is easier, to go to an extra prayer service in the hopes of pleasing God and to let him know that we really are a holy person but then grumble at the person driving too slow in front of us on the way home or to say our prayers without being showy and then pray a blessing for that person driving too slow? It's easy to say some extra prayers, but perhaps doing what is required (being good) is the more challenging thing to do. Blessed Mother Teresa of Calcutta said that we weren't called to do extraordinary things but ordinary things with great love. We don't have to go out of our way to find holiness. While all the novenas and "ornamentations" are nice, they are not necessary, nor will saying a dozen a day make us holy. If the devotions don't help us to behave more like Jesus, then what good are they? We'll have gained nothing and no one would recognize us as Christians. Jesus wants us to be good. He also knows how hard to is sometimes for us to see him in each other. Jesus has made it so easy for us to access his graces, and as Catholics we have a rich treasury to draw from. If we choose just one practice that suits us this Lent and follow it well, then it will help us in living our daily lives. Nothing is without purpose and while all the devotions may not be strictly necessary for getting us to heaven, they do have a function and can be helpful. Performing one well can help us be loving, caring, and forgiving, virtues which describe a true follower of Christ.

ANYONE OUT THERE?

It was cold. The snow lay flat on the landscape; there was no sun to make it sparkle, and the edge of the white sky and horizon blended together. The cloud of my breath hung in the air, waiting the wind's direction. The day seemed lost.

How often does our prayer seem like that? We send up a heart-felt plea to God, but the prayer just seems to hang in the air, drifting back into our faces with no one to hear. Perhaps we wonder if it's only ourselves, or if God has forgotten us? These times don't necessarily have to be great dark nights of the soul but simply dry times; there may not be any great suffering but simply emptiness.

Personally, I have a couple different ways of thinking which help me to persevere in prayer. There are times in our prayer when we have all sorts or consolations from the Holy Spirit and we are showered with graces. Those prayers are full of sweetness for us, and we would love to stay in them forever. How wonderful when we can feel God loving us so well. Thank God for those mountaintops and blessings to help us on our journey! They are needed for the dry times when we pray and nothing happens, and we feel like the above description, all empty and lifeless. Those are the times when perhaps we have a little testing from God. Of course, we want to stay with him when we feel loved; it's a comfortable, secure feeling. But what about when it's more work on our part, and we need to suffer a little? Will we stay then? Perhaps in those times, God is receiving consolations from us, not as in he's taking away gifts given us but he's receiving and feeling love and blessings from us. It cost him to love us. Why shouldn't it cost us a little to love him? Maybe he veils our eyes a little so we don't see him as well, and we hunger for him and realize how much we need him. Then when we see him again, the meeting is all the sweeter.

The other thought I had on this shows more of a failing on our parts. I know that even when my prayer is dry, God is still there and thinking of me. He's always thinking of and loving me, yet if the response to my prayer seems lacking I know it's to teach me a lesson. How often, I wonder, when God tries to speak to us, does he receive such a dry response? This is where we would fail. How often do we not even think of him and so don't hear him when he speaks? We don't respond, and he hears nothing, only emptiness. Where is God's assurance that we are still thinking of and loving him? Where does he take his comfort? May this thought spur us on to make all of our moments in his presence, not necessarily in conversation but in simply being, so we feel near each other even if no response comes.

JOYFUL SUFFERING

> The desire to receive God's treasures and favors is universal. But how few people aspire to wear themselves out and to suffer for the Son of God!
>
> —St. John of the Cross

Since I've been a bit under the weather lately, I've had a lot of time to think about the value of sickness and suffering. Considering the surprised looks I received from people when I say, "What a good offering for Lent," it seems to me that many people don't see the good that comes from illness. Not that I'm saying any illness is a desirable thing. Heavens no! It drags you down and sometimes incapacitates you to where you feel like you're just along for the ride while your body does its own thing. That's why it's called suffering. What God is anxious to see is our reaction to suffering.

Suffering could be divided into two types: that which happens to you, such as an illness, and that which you inflict on yourself, like fasting. The latter will take on different forms for every person to the degree God guides them. Fasting (or some mortification) is necessary. As in Matthew 6:16, Jesus doesn't say "*if* you fast" but "*when* you fast." However, this self-inflicted kind of suffering is more dangerous because of the extremes people take and as it can lead to the sin of pride. Undertaking any sort of penance should be done prayerfully and with wisdom. How much more valuable is simply to accept that which happens to you, not with resignation but a joyful embrace of his cross. In the words of Blessed Teresa of Calcutta, "We are at Jesus's disposal. If he wants you to be sick in bed, if he wants to you proclaim his work in the street, if he wants you to clean the toilets all day, that's all right, everything is all right. We must say, 'I belong to you. You can do whatever you like.' And this...is our strength, and this is the joy of the Lord" (Tice, n.d).

When we accept that suffering as God's will for us and entirely surrender our will to his, what a delightful perfume we send up to heaven!

While I was sick, I sent so many intentions up to our Father. I remember the words of St. Teresa of the Andes (age fifteen) when she spoke about the religious life, and it could very well apply to suffering. That "she does all this in silence with no one aware of her sacrifice… she is like the Lamb of God. She removes sin from the world. She sacrifices herself to bring back to the sheepfold those sheep who have gone astray. But just as Christ did not know the world, neither does she know it…There is no room for self-love. She doesn't even see the fruit of her prayer. In heaven alone will she know this" (Forward Boldly 2011).

So often we don't see the results of our sacrifice. We just have to trust that Jesus is using it and that someday we'll know. He needs us to continue and not give up, not feel sorry for ourselves, but to lean on him when we're tired, hold his hand a little tighter, and keep looking into his eyes, and rest assured that he'll get us through this one too.

"Jesus said to me, 'How many times would you have abandoned me, my son, if I had not crucified you. Beneath the cross, one learns love, and I do not give this to everyone, but only to those souls who are dearest to me'" (Pio 2003, 47).

BEND AND STRETCH

Deuteronomy 10:16 says, "Circumcise your hearts, therefore, and be no longer stiff-necked."

I'll be the first to admit that I can be stubborn. It runs in the family. When my Protestant grandfather married my Catholic grandmother, their families didn't make the effort to get to know each other. During that time, they had a baby boy but were so poor they had to give him up for adoption. No one knew about him for fifty-nine years until he found us, and with him came healing. Their story has a happy ending. What kind of ending do we want for our story, and what can we do to make that happen?

One way I'm stubborn is that I like certain ways of doing things (don't we all!), and I don't like to give that up. Even if I can see that it's no longer beneficial or that there's a more efficient way of doing it, I hold on to that tradition because it's what I'm used to. It's comfortable, and I like where I'm at. In this case, I must ask, "Is this my will or God's will that I'm doing now?" This is where prayer comes in. If I am so insistent that my way is the right or only way of doing something, I'm probably missing out on a chance to grow spiritually, emotionally, or mentally. What if God has something wonderful in store for me, but I miss it because I won't try a new or different thing? "For I know well the plans I have in mind for you, says the Lord, plans for your welfare, not for woe!" (Jer. 29:11). Our Father always knows what's best for me, but am I willing to bend enough to find out what it is? Do I have the courage to change something I've always done, or to change the way I pray or the way I behave? "The Lord, our God, said to us at Horeb: You have stayed long enough at this mountain. Leave here" (Deut. 1:6–7). Perhaps the mountain to leave is my own way and to discover God's way. It won't be easy because we're supposed to die in the process. "Unless a grain of wheat falls to the ground and dies, it remains just a grain of wheat; but if it dies, it produces much fruit" (John 12:24). Dying to self takes so many different forms for each one of us. Maybe for one it's not complaining or refusing to be angry or annoyed and enduring in silence like Jesus did or taking correction humbly. Perhaps it's letting go of our traditions (time to sacrifice our favorite sacrifices?) and letting God stretch us. So think and pray for the best way for Lent to prepare us for Easter this year. Perhaps the Father will lead us down new or unexpected roads. Will we be open and flexible to what he has in store for us, or will we persist in our own stubborn ways because we're sure this is the right way? May the God of all wisdom guide us this Lent.

IF I DIE

Lent has been a rather solemn time around here. In the past three weeks, my extended family has seen two sudden, unexpected deaths, each person in their forties. These events tend to put one in a different frame of mind—like what would happen if I was next? At one point, I thought I'd have to fly to St. Louis, and I was sure the plane would crash. I can honestly say that if I didn't believe in God, my thoughts would probably have bordered on hysteria. It's not death itself that bothers me, although I don't imagine I'd enjoy the act, it's those I'd leave behind that I worry about. My husband would be left with two children. I wouldn't be there to help raise them. Would they remember me? Would they know how much I loved them? These thoughts almost sent me into agony, and I wondered whether I should write them a letter just in case, so they would have something of me to hold onto. Fortunately, God is good and rescued me from my own thoughts even before I found out I didn't need to fly. I remembered it was suggested once that we could do a swap with Mary: we'd pray for her intentions and ask her to pray for ours. So I offered my whole family and our well-being up to Mary to take care of with her mother's heart in exchange for rosaries for her. The calming effect was almost instant though I do have to remind myself of the exchange sometimes.

With Jesus's death foremost in mind these days, I often wonder how he managed. He knew for certainty he was going to die. He was going to leave family and friends behind. Just one look at the Gospel of John, chapters 13–17, and we discover the love letter that Jesus left behind. It took five chapters to say goodbye to his apostles, and those chapters are full of hope, love, and consolation. Read them as if Jesus is speaking to you.

Also consider if you knew you were going to die the next day. Would your actions toward people change any? Would your words become softer or your actions gentler? Would you want the last thing you said to someone to be positive? I can only imagine what the world would be like if we tried to treasure our relationships with others and let them know it. Who knows? Maybe all it takes to heal wounds is to remember our own mortality.

THE TRIDUUM

MIRROR, MIRROR

Most time in front of mirrors is spent preening and scrutinizing our appearance as we attempt to make ourselves appear the best we can. Regardless of the flaws still underneath, we put forth a glowing surface to impress our friends.

So why is it, if we enjoy gazing into mirrors so much, we are so hesitant to look into the mirror God has given us? Jesus is the perfect, unblemished mirror by which to see our souls. But looking into our souls is hard, and by grace, we'll see what God does. When we truly see through God's eyes, we have to accuse ourselves of wrongdoings, either intentional or unintentional. It takes a lot of guts to stand up and admit that yes, I'm the one who caused your sorrow when it's so much easier to turn our face and imagine the flaw isn't there.

During the Last Supper, Jesus tells his apostles that one of them would surely betray him. John leans back to Jesus and looks into his face and asks, "Is it I, Lord?" How daring! Such a powerful question. Do we have the courage to look into the face of Jesus or our family and friends and ask that question? What if Jesus says yes? Is it I, Lord?

Thanks be to God that Jesus is a merciful God. When we gaze into his face and ask about our faults, we look not only into the face of the just judge but of our Savior. God has four main attributes, those being his holiness and justice and, now especially, his love and mercy. Through the sacrament of confession, he gave us an opportunity to rectify the wrongs done and clean up our souls before that mirror. So many people don't use the chance he gave. They know if they were to ask what John asked, the answer might be yes, and they don't want to face that. The devil deters people from confession by giving them back something he took away before: shame. But Jesus himself says not to be afraid. He told St. Faustina in messages for the world, When you go to confession, to this fountain of my mercy, the blood and water which came forth from my heart always flows down upon your soul (St. Kowalska 1990, 1602). I am love and mercy itself (1074). Let no soul fear to draw near to me, even though its sins be as scarlet (699). My Mercy is greater than your sins and those of the entire world (1485). I let my sacred heart be pierced with a lance, thus opening wide the source of mercy for you. Come, then, with trust to draw graces from this fountain. I would never reject a contrite heart (1485).

Let's not be afraid then, as Lent draws to a conclusion, to examine our souls before the mirror of God and take advantage of the wonderful opportunity he has given us. No, admitting something wrong is never easy, but perhaps we can take courage from St. John who did lean back to Jesus, look into his face, and ask, "Is it I, Lord?"

BETRAYED

"Mother!" John gasped as Mary tripped and nearly fell headlong into the ground. Darkness covered the road; it was difficult to see. They were hurrying, Mary practically dragging John along to the temple area where the guards had taken Jesus. John had run straight from the Garden of Gethsemane to where Mary was staying with friends and told her. Told her what? That Jesus had been taken, betrayed by one of his own apostles? John couldn't even remember what he'd said. He was so shocked by Judas's sudden appearance in the garden with the guard. Judas was one of them! He was their friend or had been. John's stomach twisted at the look on Jesus's face. Disappointment? Sorrow? How agonizing to discover a friend wasn't really a friend after all. But Jesus had known, had foretold it at the Passover meal. Knowledge didn't make the reality any easier. At the house, between John's mumbled words and the look on his face, Mary simply grabbed his hand and ran.

THE CHOICES WE MAKE

"[Senior devil Screwtape to junior devil Wormwood:] Desiring their freedom, he [God] therefore refuses to carry them, by their mere affections and habits, to any of the goals which he sets before them: he leaves them to 'do it on their own.' And there lies our opportunity. But also, remember, there lies our danger. If once they get through this initial dryness successfully, they become much less dependent on emotion and therefore much harder to tempt" (Martindale and Root 1989, 161).

Webster's Dictionary defines *will* as "choice, determination; the power of control over one's own actions or emotions." During Holy Week, I found myself making a rather odd comparison (or contrast), that of Judas Iscariot and Blessed Mother Teresa of Calcutta, in regards to free will. Both of them were overwhelmed with intense dark emotion and thoughts; one succumbed to evil and the other chose light. Judas, when he regretted his actions deeply (Matt. 27:3), was filled with remorse over his sin. He could have turned to God and begged forgiveness. Instead, he allowed despair (a far greater sin because you're giving up hope in God) to enter his soul, which cost him his life. Mother Teresa, on the other hand, also experienced severe darkness in her soul as indicated by her letters: "There is so much contradiction in my soul. Such deep longing for God—so deep that it is painful—a suffering continual—and yet not wanted by God—repulsed—empty—no faith—no love—no zeal...Pray for me please that I keep smiling at him in spite of everything" (Mother Teresa, 169).

But rather than surrender to the crushing misery of feeling unwanted by God, she chose to trust God in her darkness—an act of sheer will—even saying that she would go on like this forever if it makes him happy. So now I wonder how many of us go through our lives being swayed by our thoughts and emotions rather than clinging to the rock of a will that is determined to place all hope on God?

So many things assail our souls these days, but perhaps the most dangerous is our own emotions. We've become a touchy-feely world with *me* at the center. How many marriages, vocations, or lives are lost this way? Our human hearts are fickle, and emotions constantly change, so dare we let them be our guide? Even our thoughts cannot be sure guideposts as spiritual matters make no rational sense to the world. Did it make sense for Mother Teresa—living in such pain, physically and spiritually—to continue her life as a nun? Yet she did. What must be our guide is our faith that which defies both emotion and reason. When we have darkness in our soul, do we give in to defeat like Judas? Instead, we must hold on to the hope Jesus gives. We must do all we can to realize that if God's hiding his face for a while, it's only so that we will lift our heads and look for him. When Mother Teresa looked for Jesus, she could find him only in the faces of the poor. She willed herself to hold on to that revelation even when her emotions rebelled. Wherever it is we find God, we need to hold onto him with all our might, or we may find ourselves going the way of Judas.

THY WILL BE DONE

Imagine Jesus in the Garden of Gethsemane, praying before his betrayal. Regarding his upcoming passion, Jesus prays "Father...take this cup away from me" (Mark 14:36). Rightfully, we think that he speaks about his death. Who would willingly undergo what Jesus did for us and not sweat blood? But consider this, Jesus is God and could have walked away from the whole thing. He could have disappeared through the soldiers and lived out his life peacefully somewhere. Instead, he wrestled with himself that night to subdue his own will. "Father, let this cup (my wanting my own way, of my wanting to be in control) let that cup pass from me." Perhaps a portion of "this cup" then would be his indecisiveness. Let this cup of my hesitation pass so that I may embrace your will fully. Then he won. He surrendered to his Father, "But not what I will but what you will."

He surrendered his will, not just leaving emptiness and passively accepting whatever might come his way but actively embracing his Father's. God doesn't want just an empty shell, a robot to do what he says. He wants a person, heart, mind and soul, to desire Him and His way. To say to our Father, "I desire You more than I desire me," is like music. How many times a day do we want our own way, do we make decisions even in the littlest things without consulting God? Yet when he hears us say "I surrender" to any decision, and then a minute later have to surrender again to the same matter because we want something different, each time is like an arrow of love in his heart for us, humbling him that we would desire him so. Our Father is overjoyed when his creatures love him. Therefore, he only has our best interests in mind—interests from heaven's point of view and not our limited perspective here on earth. He will mold us into his image (that of perfect love) with crucifixion marks and all. We cannot expect any less. Why would we want to?

FIAT

For all the crowds that Mary had been in, when thousands of people jostled to hear Jesus, nothing frightened her like standing in this crowd. It rumbled like an angry lion, waiting to pounce. Her head ached, probably from the events of the night and morning. How many places had they dragged Jesus, more beaten each time she saw Him? Annas, Caiaphas, the Sanhedrin, Pilate, Herod, then back to Pilate, oh! He looked so weary and bruised. Her mother's heart kept pleading, Now that he's been scourged, please, let him go. Isn't it enough? But another part knew they wouldn't. Then Pilate's voice thundered out "Behold, the man!" Mary looked and started to cry out Jesus's name, but it stuck in her throat. She pressed her hands against her mouth, and a whimper escaped. Jesus stood, not an inch of him clear of blood, cloaked in purple and what was that? Thorns? Someone had woven a crown from a thorny branch and pushed it into his head. "My son!" Mary whispered and sagged against John. She heard the chief priests and guards debating back and forth with Pilate, but she couldn't take her eyes off her only child. "Crucify him, crucify him!" Mary's breath caught and she thought wildly, What? Oh God, please no! Jesus, oh my Jesus. Please, melt away through the crowd. Leave this place. Oh please, just leave. But deep down in her heart, a leaden word resounded through her soul, Yes. She had said yes, all those years ago. Yes to a message brought by an angel that she would have

God's Son. Yes to shepherds' visits, yes to exile in Egypt. Yes to all those quiet, joyful years in Nazareth raising Jesus, yes even to Joseph's death. Yes, Mary traveled with Jesus as much as she could during his ministry, and now again at what was to be his death, yes. It had cost her dearly. It was all she could give. Yes, Father, if this horror is your plan, then so be it. Mary dropped her face into her hands. Yes.

OUR OWN YES

Mary embraced the will of God whole-heartedly regardless of whether obedience meant joy or the mourning of a mother's heart. What did her yes allow? Jesus came to reconcile the world to his Father through his own obedience and to heal what had been broken. His own humble submission to the will of God repaired what disobedience and pride lost long ago. For Mary, the yes was a complete surrender of a mother's rights when she offered up on the pure altar of her Immaculate Heart the sacrifice of her son. The cost was great, yet both Jesus and Mary said, "Behold, I come to do your will, O God" (Heb. 10:7). What of us? Can we lean back, comfortable in the knowledge the sacrifice was made and accepted for us? Could we claim no responsibilities and simply enjoy the reward? No. If we want to be called Christians, then we've the duty to obey him whose commands we claim to follow. This requires heart-to-heart knowledge of God, for how can we obey his will if we don't know what his will is? Three wills need discernment: the will of the evil one, which leads away from God; the fallen human will, which is selfish by nature; and the will of God, which leads to salvation with him. Only through prayer and more prayer can we come to know, love, and praise God with our whole heart and begin to align our will with his. God's will can be both joy and sacrifice as Jesus and Mary have shown us, but the peace that comes from following him is unsurpassed. We gain our strength from God's peace. Then regardless of the action, whether it's our daily duties or a more courageous undertaking, we can truly say, "Here I am, Lord, I come to do your will."

GRACE FREELY GIVEN

It isn't so hard to imagine our world dying, pierced by Satan's sword, and Mary doing everything she can to help us. Finally, she cries out to the Father, "What grace you gave to me, let it pass to them!" Ah, now it comes to this. Will we accept that grace? Do we truly want to live? If we accept God's grace, then we must live by that grace. Mary said yes, and she was made full of grace; every aspect of her character was infused by it, and she surrendered her life completely to him. Her relationship to God was so intense that she uniquely joined in Jesus's passion on the cross and was sustained by that grace.

Humility made our Lady well-disposed to receive God's grace in its entirety. Only a humble heart—which recognizes that we are what we are and which admits that there is one greater than us in all things—can accept his grace. His grace is our life, the sweet breath of God breathed into us, which gives strength to the weary and hope to all. We need only ask for it. How generous a God who gives such a gift when simply asked! So powerful and gentle. His grace warms us when no fire can. And when our Lord's grace comes, we see how weak and broken we are without it. What thank-yous our souls cry when we see how Jesus took our place and, with his broken body, clasped us in his arms and cried, "What grace is mine, let it be yours! ("I came so that they might have life and have it more abundantly" [John 10:10]). We are so powerless without his grace.

During this Lent, let us join ourselves with Mary at the foot of Jesus's cross. The same grace that held Mary during Jesus's passion is available to us. When life sometimes seems so hard that we just won't make it through, ask Mary as our mediatrix of grace to pour that grace upon us. Ask for grace in good times and bad; we need it in every situation. To accept God's grace means surrendering our lives completely to him. We need to let go, to allow ourselves to be annihilated in the perfecting flames of his love and mercy. "My grace is sufficient for you, for power is made perfect in weakness" (2 Cor. 12:9). His grace is our strength, and when we do everything by his grace, it's for his glory. Living by God's grace is very humbling, but it's what he calls us to. Now we must decide. Can we do it? Life is his gift to us. Do we want to truly live?

FOCUS

Breathe, just breathe.

My stomach cramped up that fast. I was sitting at the computer, fine one minute and the next, I was staggering to my bedroom, hunched over, with the world going black before my eyes. My head swam, and I didn't know if I was going to pass out or be sick. Fortunately, I was neither, but for two hours, I was immobilized by pain from endometriosis. During that time, I couldn't really think straight. I only knew I wanted the pain to stop. Occasionally, I remembered that I should be offering it for the souls in purgatory or in reparation for sins. Mostly though, I simply repeated, "Jesus, Jesus," over and over. I could picture his face, so I just looked into his eyes and focused on them. He's always gotten me through no matter what the predicament I've been in; I can always focus on his face in the darkness.

I've often wondered when Jesus was on the cross and the pain was overwhelming, what did he focus on? For parts of his passion, his mother was right there before his eyes. It would only make sense to focus on his mama. Interiorly, I'm sure Jesus focused also on his Father. Their love for each other is beyond understanding, the love that drew Jesus to obey his Father's will. God willed for us to be reconciled to him, and Jesus knew his own death and resurrection would bring that about. So Jesus willingly did the unthinkable, and he sacrificed himself for love of his Father, for love of us. So was Jesus thinking of and looking at us as well? Do I dare to imagine that for perhaps the tiniest split second, Jesus might have had my face in his focus too? (The presumption of such a thought!) And yet in that thought I can find inspiration as well, to hope that when Jesus thought of me, he could see me loving him. Maybe that thought inspires me in weak moments to make better choices or to put extra effort into my work if it will ease Jesus's pain a tiny bit. If, for any reason, Jesus focused on me, then I want that glimpse to give him comfort, and perhaps I can make up for some of the suffering he endured for me.

Whatever it is we've decided to do for Lent, there are times when it won't be easy. Think of Jesus during those times, and now turn the focus the other way too. Try to imagine Jesus looking at you and loving you, so much so that he's gone to the other side of death and back for you. Then it won't matter whether you succeed in that particular mortification or not. What matters is that you've kept your eyes on Jesus. Just you and him, he and you loving each other through everything forever.

A GIFT FROM JESUS

I get frustrated at times with people who are pessimistic when I want them to know that there's hope beyond whatever their situation is. It's rather like telling people who are standing in a dark room that there's light; all they have to do is flip the switch. But what is light to them if they don't know what light is? Why should they believe there's such a thing as light? How did the apostles convince people that there was such a thing as God and that he made a difference in their lives? Why has he given me the grace to know him and not them? I love this hope that our faith gives us. This hope is what's gotten me through every single trial in my life as I can honestly say that, without it, I probably wouldn't be here. I've kept as a mantra in my mind what St. Julian of Norwich said, "All shall be well, and all shall be well and all manner of thing shall be well" (Kiefer, n.d.). In all honesty, trials will come no matter what our disposition. Even though we are children of the light, we walk in a world covered in darkness, and that darkness seeps into our lives. Seeing his light won't take away the aching and agony steeped in our hearts; the sadness remains. But if there's sadness with nothing beyond it, what's to keep us from despairing? The light gives us something to hold onto when our hearts are breaking into pieces and we're sure that things will never be okay again. It helps us answer the question of how do we survive this? The answer is that alone, we don't. God survives it in and for us. Jesus is the "light [that] shines in the darkness, and the darkness has not overcome it" (John 1:5). Jesus himself said, "In the world you will have trouble, but take courage, I have conquered the world" (John 16:33). So why should I trust in Jesus? I trust because he did it first. He went through everything first. Did even Jesus's faith waver on the cross when he cried out, "My God, my God, why have you forsaken me?" (Matt. 27:46), calling his Father "God" for the first and last time in his life. Jesus's faith held out as he cried out in a loud voice (a shout of defiance to temptation?), "Father, into your hands I commend my spirit" (Luke 23:46), showing us that he still believed his Father was there, that his Father would still receive his spirit. Jesus died, but death didn't win. When Jesus rose again, he proved that everything he said was true. God our Father exists. He's waiting for us to fulfill our mission, to love the best we can, to hold on to him the best we can through every trial. Then when God chooses and not before, we'll go home to him. If I can keep that attitude Jesus had, the hope that Jesus had, that will make all the difference in how I view the trials in my life. I pray, pray, pray that somehow he will help me convey that hope to others who are in such desperate need of it as well.

BATTLEFRONT

The bumper sticker on a car passing by read "Jesus was a pacifist." *Webster's Dictionary* states that a *pacifist* is someone who is "strongly and actively opposed to conflict and especially war." Okay, Jesus was always saying to turn the other cheek and offer the other as well (Matt. 5:39). I guess that could be taken for pacifism. He didn't resist the soldiers' torments leading up to and including the crucifixion. Then I had to ask why, why didn't he resist them? What was the point Jesus was making? And it was so obvious: he was fighting a battle! He was being obedient and countering the evil with good. He was fighting for the obedience and humility taken away in the Garden of Eden. Jesus had free will; he could have said no, but instead, he chose steadfast, painful obedience to make right what Adam did wrong. So how was this defeating Satan? Jesus didn't mean to turn away when someone does evil to you; that just allows evil to spread and flourish. He means to combat it with the good, counter it by doing what is right. Jesus died for the truth. Do we have the courage to face evil and do good despite it all?

When I taught CCD (Confraternity of Christian Doctrine), I used to tell my high school students that we were on the frontlines of a war. God exists whether we want him to or not. The devil exists as well. It's been said that the devil's greatest accomplishment is to make us believe he doesn't exist. There are no absolute right and wrongs anymore; morality is a matter of personal opinion. Sound familiar? Is the devil winning? The stakes are high. The property being fought for is our souls. We are the frontlines. Jesus also said, "Do not think that I have come to bring peace upon earth. I have come to bring not peace but the sword" (Matt. 10:34). He doesn't want us to remain complacent while injustice and wickedness flourish around us. Pacifism will avoid war at any cost, even at the cost of our souls. Jesus has already won the war for us through his death and resurrection. We are no longer slaves; he has freed us from the burden of guilt, and we need to live in that freedom. What will we choose? Will we have the courage to fight evil and retaliate with good? Or will we continue to let sin dominate our lives through compromise just to pacify and soothe any ruffled feathers? Our Lord Jesus Christ, in obedience, suffered and died for the truth. For which side will we choose to fight?

Mary closed her eyes in remembrance: she was holding her babe on her lap, and his thumb wrapped tightly around hers. His head was still so wobbly! It kind of bobbed back and forth, but little Jesus's eyes remained locked on hers as he blew smiley raspberries.

Mary was jolted out of her reverie when John touched her shoulder; she looked down at Jesus's lifeless body in her arms. She had been rocking him, her leaden arms wrapped around Jesus's cooling body as she leaned her chin on top of his head. She rocked him and her tears spilled forth. "O God, help me now."

EASTER

A SACRAMENT OF HOPE

It's been said that if we are comfortable reading the Bible, then we are reading it wrong. It's meant to challenge us, to make us step out of our convenient lives and grow along the way of Jesus. The same could almost be said about the holy Mass, in particular the services during Holy Week. One line comes to mind actually, because it forces us to look at ourselves. The line "Crucify him!" We like to think of ourselves as good people, and in truth, we are. All of God's creation is good. But we are also fallen, and because of our fallen nature, we can't help but sin. The magnitude of that sin depends on our relationship with God; even the mystic can see the faintest blemish on her soul and is humbled. So when we read the passion and cry out as the crowd, "Crucify him, crucify him!" we must admit in our hearts that we mean that. Oh, it's nice to think that we would be different. We would never abandon him or cry out with the crowd condemning Jesus. We would be right there even to the foot of the cross. Yet every time we sin, isn't shouting "Crucify him" exactly what we're doing? We abandon Jesus for another way. We add to his wounds with our willful disobedience, and we crucify him again. His sacrifice on Calvary ought to challenge us in the Mass as well. The Mass may be a bloodless sacrifice, but the pain of our sins is still felt by Jesus. If we could see Jesus in the Eucharist and how he comes to us and how unthinking we come to him with our sins, how much more would we take care of our souls! We'd run for the confessional, so our sins would not stain the pure beauty, that divine goodness, of Jesus when we receive him in communion. And yet the sacrifice on Calvary must go on. Who is there to crucify Jesus today? If we haven't reconciled ourselves to him through confession, then it is we who play the part of the disdaining crowds. Even an unconfessed priest, whose hands hold Jesus in the consecrated bread, plays the Roman soldiers. But the Eucharist is a sacrament of hope. In the Eucharist, Jesus makes all things new. "Upon him was the chastisement that makes us whole, by his stripes we were healed" (Isa. 53:5). Jesus gave his life out of love and desire for us, in the hope that we would find our way back to him and love him. That alone should give us the courage and humility to bow before God and say, "Have mercy on me, a sinner!" Invite Mary into our hearts and go to him with her heart. Jesus came to his mother despite her squalid stable surroundings at his birth. He will come to his mother living in our hearts. They will purify us. Then with a new heart and hope, we can look to our Savior and say thank you.

The new covenant

We have just finished Holy Week; we have heard the words Jesus spoke echoed in the Mass,

> "FOR THIS IS THE CHALICE OF MY **BLOOD**
> THE **BLOOD** OF THE NEW AND ETERNAL
> CONVENANT WHICH WILL BE POURED
> OUT FOR YOU AND FOR MANY FOR THE
> FORGIVENESS OF SINS."

By now we understand that he meant those words literally. But do we understand all the words? What about the new covenant part? Just what is the new covenant that Jesus was so intent on ratifying? What are its terms?

God starts his salvation history with Adam and Eve, our first parents. He continues through Noah and his family, reestablishing the original covenant and stating that he will never again destroy humanity by flood. Next comes the covenant with Abraham where God extends his contract, gives Abraham his own land and says that he will be a great nation (Gen. 12). The Sinaitic covenant is the application of Abraham's covenant to the whole nation. After leaving Egypt (Exod. 19:5–6) by giving the law to Moses, God establishes

Israel as a national unit with a specific set of laws, not just an ethnic group. Later, the Davidic covenant (2 Sam.7: 8–16) establishes a family line through David. A reference is also made to someone having God as a Father. Notice how God's narrowing his focus—first, humanity then Israel then a remnant. Finally, having broken the Sinaitic covenant, the people are confronted with the destruction of Jerusalem. On the eve of this attack by the Babylonians, Jeremiah calls out a new covenant, the one to which Jesus (who is the focal point of history) refers. In Jeremiah 31:31–34, God says that he will make a new covenant with Israel: "I will place my law within them, and write it upon their hearts; I will be their God, and they shall be my people. No longer will they have need to teach their friends and kinsmen how to know the Lord. All, from least to greatest, shall know me, says the Lord, for I will forgive their evildoing and remember their sin no more."

It's a wonderful covenant of mercy! However, it was never ratified because the people were led off to Babylonian exile. In order for a covenant to be sealed, it must be ratified by the blood of an animal, such as a lamb, and the sacrifice completed in the meal. Jesus becomes the focal point of history by becoming the spotless Lamb of God, his body sacrificed on the cross, and blood poured out for us, becoming the Eucharist. Every time we consume Jesus in the host, we are continuing the sacrificial meal and renewing the covenant with God. What a covenant to renew! To have the law written in our hearts, to have personal intimacy with God and, most of all, to have forgiveness! Jesus is truly our merciful Savior, the means by which our redemption takes place. In his mission, Jesus preached first to his disciples (the remnant). The disciples went to Israel and then to all humanity, bringing us finally back to God. The question now is whether we'll accept or refuse our part in the new covenant. Our Father only wants what's best for us, but he never promised the way would be easy. Will we choose to live the life Jesus proposes and imitate our Savior? Keep the Bible close at hand, it's the guidebook God gave us; stay close to the church, it's the gift Jesus died for to give us; study, pray, and discover his truth.

OFFERING OURSELVES

The past couple of years, I've had an opportunity to present the story of *The Giving Tree* by Shel Silverstein to early elementary classes. Afterwards, I ask them to tell me things that they can give to someone that come from the heart and that don't necessarily cost money. Last year's class came up with a plethora of ideas. This year's class was like pulling teeth. They were very material-oriented. However, after a while, they eventually got the idea, and then they wanted to give everything away! They even caught on that such a simple thing as listening to their teacher in class could be a gift to her. It was nice, seeing the change.

To another class, I presented the idea that God has given us many gifts, but the most important gift was Jesus. Through Jesus, we learn the way back to our Father in heaven; we learn how he wants us to live. Then I asked, what was Jesus's gift to us? One little girl actually came up with the answer: his body and blood in the Eucharist. Not bad for a third grader. Jesus's gift to us was to open the gates of heaven and to be with us always and everywhere. How simple an idea, and how profound in application. If only we could all see as clearly as the children! But because we know the cost involved, that the Father sacrificed his Son, the Son sacrificed his life, we shrink from it. So dear is God's love for us that, at first glance, we are terrified by it; and then when we willingly continue to gaze at him, we allow ourselves to be annihilated in that sacrificial love, and so breathe in the cold air of our call. We offer ourselves to become his instruments so that others may know the joy of his love as well. Once we've experienced his true love, we accept that there will be sacrifices if we want to give his love away to others. We don't always know what those sacrifices will be. The gift will fit the situation. Perhaps at times we can offer the gift gladly, or perhaps it will be demanded of us. Whatever the need is, God will supply the strength to see us through and bring us closer to him.

Perhaps in this Easter season, we can consider what we could offer God. I think of the story of the widow putting in her two coins, and it being all she had to offer. "I cannot offer to the Lord, my God, holocausts that cost nothing" (2 Sam. 24:24). What do I give him out of my necessity? My time in prayer? Cheerfulness in doing routine, menial tasks? Proclaiming his message of love to unreceptive audiences? Patience in family life? Everyone will have their own gift, and it will be unique. What will our gift be?

WAITING

It's Holy Saturday afternoon, and finally, the sun is shining. Some birds are singing outside; a nice change from the heaviness of the rain yesterday. The church services are all done, now we wait. Is this what it was like after the horribleness of the first Good Friday? In our present time, we find things to fill our day: baking, decorating, and readying the house, waiting for Easter vigil. But what about the first disciples? Did they wait, anticipating, or for them was their life with Jesus done? Jesus had said, "Come, follow me," but now he had gone where they could not follow. What was left? Mary knew. She was one of the few, if any, who believed there was more and waited in silence. How agonizingly long was that wait for her? Could it have been only yesterday that she lived an eternity under that cross? Her son, her God was up there bleeding. How could God bleed? Yet there he was, confounding the wisdom of the sages. O my God, my God is dying. How could God die? Come, follow me. So there must be more, right? What does it mean to follow him? So now she waits and ponders all this in her heart. She waits, and the world in stillness waits with her.

Now we're waiting for the vigil. We know, in hindsight, that Jesus rises, and we're anxious to get to Easter. It isn't easy going through all the fasting and remembering the passion he suffered, but that's why he came to earth. We need time to consider the scope of these events. God's love isn't always warm and gentle (as much as we might like to think so), Sometimes, it purifies and heals. How was our Father to heal this rift between us and him? How else but to send his Son, an agreement between themselves, to mend what we could not? He would be obedient when we were not. So today we need to stand with Mary at the foot of the cross and ponder it a little, ponder that Jesus said, "Come, follow me," and this was the road he chose. Our Father God bent down from heaven and chose to become like us, who spend a good bit of our lives in trial and suffering. Ah, our first clue to how we follow him: bend down. Be little, be humble. If we are humble, then we are patient. In patience, we'll learn how not simply to endure suffering but to make it our joyful offering to him and to unite completely with him. Jesus gave our lives meaning by showing us how to suffer, and then how to lay down our lives for each other in love. Come, follow me. This is only the beginning. There's so much more. Ours is a God whose love is unfathomable. He'll take our little hands in his strong ones, scarred by the nails, and show us the way. We'll get through Good Friday and the quiet Holy Saturday, patiently walking with him and following him to Easter.

ALMOST THERE

There's just something about Holy Week and Easter that defies explanation. It exudes an air of sacredness, anticipation, and fervent desire for unity with him who died for us. Yes, personally, Easter is my favorite time of the year. Through the Holy Week services, I can catch a small glimpse of the magnitude of our Father's plan, and I do mean just a glimpse. If we truly had any idea of God's intentions, then the churches would be packed year round.

During the Easter vigil, there's a moment that for me says, "Breathe again. Celebrate. Jesus is rising soon!" when the "Glory to God" is sung with full voices, the lights are flipped on, and bells are ringing. "Zeal for your house consumed me" (Ps. 69:10). Jesus is coming in the Eucharist! Come quickly! I pray that this zeal is spread to every soul and every heart set on fire with love. All Jesus waits for is our yes. If we allow him, he will come and consume us in the Eucharist. St. Augustine said that we become what we eat. When we eat food, that food becomes part of us. It is consumed. But when we eat the Eucharist, we are consumed; we become the Body of Christ. How wonderful, how beautiful God is! We need to be amazed at the Eucharist, we need to be amazed that the glory of God can shine through us, and we need to be amazed that God should love us so much as to die to take away our sin. There are so many things that this world tries to wow us with these days. Let us not forget to be wowed by a Father taking his children in his arms and loving them. He wants to be one with us. Jesus said so (John 17:21). I've heard it said by some that they would love the Easter vigil if only there weren't so many baptisms and such to go through. But again, this is one of those moments—people choosing to follow a new way, God's way of life. Not only the elect can prepare for a new life with Jesus during Lent, we can too. If baptism signifies conversion, then we all need to be silently renewing our baptismal vows. What more is conversion than a desire to be with God? Let that zeal for his house give us the strength to take on the trials of life with passion and to firmly believe that our sacrifices mean something. Each time we embrace the cross with Jesus, we step that much closer to heaven. We need only to lift up our hands, and our Father will bend down the rest of the way for us. That is how much his zeal for us is, that he would send his only Son (John 3:16). Our trials purify us so that we can see how much more we need to come clean before facing him. As our desire for God grows, so will our desire for prayer and our distaste of sin. The Holy Spirit will help us in whatever way necessary, as the need arises, to bring others and ourselves closer to God. We only need not be afraid. "For God did not give us a spirit of cowardice…do not be ashamed of your testimony to our Lord" (2 Tim. 1: 7–8). There's so much to Holy Week. Allow yourself to be amazed.

RESURRECTION

Was she really hugging her son? Her mind stopped questioning. Yes. Mary cried into his shoulder, weeping at the tumult of events and emotions over the past couple of days. It was almost too much to take in, yet here Jesus was—real, alive, his embrace so tight it nearly lifted her off the ground.

According to *Webster's Dictionary*, *hope* is "desire accompanied by expectation of or belief in fulfillment." That definition alone implies faith. Neither faith nor hope can be contained in a world where everything is seen. To the nonbeliever, this very Easter season is illogical in what we celebrate—the resurrection of Jesus from the dead, the hope that there is life after death. Yet that is what Jesus gives us. That hope is what gives us the courage to look beyond what could be the drudgery of life.

There are times when it might be impossible to explain to an unbeliever what it is we hope for, as all we have to go by are Jesus's words and actions. Even Mary, who contemplated all the events of Jesus's life in her heart, might have wondered what it meant to rise from the dead. Nowhere in the gospels does it mention the meeting between Jesus and his mother after his resurrection. Can we even imagine the joy of that reunion? After experiencing the agony of her son's death, Mary could only wait in hope for that mysterious *third day* when Jesus would rise again. Oh, what unspeakable joy to look into his eyes and hold him in her arms again! How glorious to have that hope revealed!

Mary and all who saw Jesus were given concrete assurance of their belief in him. We, however, must once again go by faith. We trust in his teachings. At times though, our trials can still seem almost unbearable. Perhaps the hardest trial is, even now, that of death because we are separated from our loved ones.

"We also groan within ourselves as we wait for...the redemption of our bodies. For in hope we were saved. Now hope that sees for itself is not hope. For who hopes for what one sees? But if we hope for what we do not see, we wait with endurance" (Rom. 8:23–25). Someday, by God's grace, we will be together again, and we will have the reunion that Jesus and Mary had. Each day brings us closer to those who went before us. That's part of the wonderful gift Jesus gave us at Easter—life with him in heaven. Eternity with our Father. Since the saints are with him in heaven and we live in him and he in us, we are together always. So let us try, ever so earnestly, to use the patient endurance that God, in his grace, gives us and live in the joyful hope to which Jesus calls us. Christ is risen. Alleluia!

THE FEAST OF DIVINE MERCY

On May 23, 2000, the universal church was granted permission by Pope St. John Paul II to celebrate the Feast of Divine Mercy as requested by Jesus through his servant, St. Faustina Kowalska. If only everyone could know of this beautiful day when the floodgates of heaven burst open for anyone who asks! Jesus said,

> Tell the whole world about My inconceivable mercy. I desire that the Feast of Mercy be a refuge and shelter for all souls, and especially for poor sinners. On that day the very depths of My tender mercy are open. I pour out a whole ocean of graces upon those souls who approach the fount of My mercy. The soul that will go to Confession and receive Holy Communion shall obtain complete forgiveness of sins and punishment. On that day all the divine floodgates through which grace flow are opened. Let no soul fear to draw near to Me, even though its sins be as scarlet. My mercy is so great that no mind, be it of man or of angel, will be able to fathom it throughout all eternity. Everything that exists has come forth from the very depths of My most tender mercy. Every soul in its relation to Me will contemplate My love and mercy through-out eternity. The Feast of Mercy emerged from My very depths of tenderness. It is My desire that it be solemnly celebrated on the first Sunday after Easter. Mankind will not have peace until it turns to the Fount of My Mercy. (St. Kowalska 1990, 699)

GO TO YOUR ROOM

"Girls! Stop it! That's it, go to your rooms. Now!" I clenched my hands in exasperation, considering their latest antics while trying to calm down. How many times I have bitten my tongue to keep from yelling at my children, I couldn't tell you. It amazes me that someone I love so much manages to try my patience so often. Later as I prayed about that whole scenario and my reaction to it, I thought, Oh, the lessons God keeps throwing at me! What a wonderful lesson on his mercy! There are several prayers in which we plead with Christ, "Within your wounds, hide me." This particular one being from the Anima Christi. I've always wondered about that strange request and exactly what it meant. I understand the next line, "Let me not be separate from you," but why so close as to be within his wounds? Was it so that we might share uniquely in the suffering of Christ? That could be the explanation, but I wasn't happy with that. A combination of dealing with my daughters and seeing the current actions of humanity have given me an explanation I like better.

The world today commits so many atrocities against our Lord. We are like children who've angered their Father. So when we've done something that cuts us off from God, the only thing left to do is to plead for his mercy. Oh, thank heavens, our God is a merciful God! He will hide us in the wounds of Christ, whom he loves, until his anger has passed. (Rather like being sent to our room, isn't it?) Yes, we will have to deal with the due justice of God as would any children who've earned discipline, but he will wait until his indignation has cooled.

During this Easter season and celebrating the Feast of Divine Mercy, the sacrifice that Jesus made for us is especially vivid. Through participating in his sacrifice by means of the Mass, we are healed. We can live a good life according to the gospel, and we'll have still done only what God asks of us. Our fallen humanity remains. It's only by the blood of Jesus and his plea for mercy that we are saved. Take up his plea and beg for God's healing mercy to rain on the whole world!

> O Jesus! Deep abyss of mercy! I beg of thee, in memory of thy wounds which penetrated to the very marrow of thy bones and to the depth of thy being, to draw me, a miserable sinner, overwhelmed by my offenses, away from sin, and to hide me from

thy face justly irritated against me, hide me in thy wounds until thy anger and just indignation have passed away. Amen.

—Prayers of St. Bridget of Sweden

OF MERCY AND FORGIVENESS

"Another mystery of light is the preaching by which Jesus proclaims the coming of the kingdom of God, calls to conversion and forgives the sins of all who draw near to him in humble trust: the inauguration of that ministry of mercy which he continues to exercise until the end of the world"

(John Paul II, 2002, sec. 21).

What is it that more than anything defines Jesus's ministry? Was it the healings or the miracles? Perhaps the parables or the meals he shared, his crucifixion and resurrection? But what are they all about? Above all, Jesus's ministry to us can be defined through mercy and forgiveness. He spoke about forgiveness even more than he spoke about love. So what does he say about mercy?

The scriptures are so full of references to God mercy; it's hard to select just one verse. Perhaps Ephesians 2:1–10 is as good a place as any. St. Paul states that all which is ours by right, all we have earned is God's wrath (verse 3). But verse 4 says that God is rich in mercy, and verse 8, that mercy is his gift to us, his favor to us is the salvation that's ours through faith. There is absolutely no way we could've earned his mercy; it's God's free gift to us. But what is mercy? Mercy is forgiveness that we don't deserve. It's what got the Pharisees and other leaders so mad at Jesus. Jesus said that all people could come to him freely, without cost, to find rest and forgiveness in him. "Come, without paying and without cost, drink wine and milk!" (Isa. 55:1).

"Let him turn to the Lord for mercy; to our God, who is generous in forgiving" (Isa. 55:7). Only a humble soul is capable of receiving grace; a proud heart has no room for God. But the Pharisees said there were standards, rules to be followed, and if someone broke the law they should be punished. Jesus was breaking those rules, and the people loved him for it. No wonder he drew divided crowds.

Jesus would've been a great lawyer. He did put one contingency in the Lord's Prayer, and it's not in our relationship to God but to others: forgive us our trespasses as we forgive those who trespass against us. It's the only line of the prayer that he emphasizes afterwards. "If you forgive others their transgressions, your heavenly Father will forgive you. But if you do not forgive others, neither will your Father forgive your transgressions" (Matt. 6:14–15). It comes down to this: we cannot receive what we're unwilling to give, and we cannot give what we're unwilling to receive. When we submit completely to the Father, we realize that he can forgive all sins. "Come to me heedfully, listen, that you may have life" (Isa. 55:3). The only thing God requires of us is to acknowledge him as God. Come to him in humble prayer and thus imitate him by forgiving others. Carrying a burden of guilt within ourselves isn't necessary. Jesus offers us complete freedom. From this freedom comes the ability to live the life of God within us—to be merciful when our human nature can't, to show God's love when we've reached our limits. This unconditional forgiveness is our primary gift from God. When we recognize the gift, when we've fallen on our faces in humility, adoration, and gratitude, then we can continue the work of Jesus and proclaim the kingdom of God.

Later on in the same chapter of Isaiah 55, verse 8, God tells us, "For my thoughts are not your thoughts, nor are my ways your ways, says the Lord." Nor is his time our time. It is my own belief that this time of mercy has lasted so long that we no longer recognize his mercy. We are not aware of the torrential graces being poured upon us. So when God's day of justice comes, I think his mercy will come to a stark, sudden end if only to make us aware of how great his mercy was.

"Tell souls about this great mercy of Mine, because the awful day, the day of My justice, is near (St. Kowalska 1990, 965). Before the Day of Justice, I am sending the Day of Mercy (1588)...I am pro-longing the time of mercy for the sake of sinners. But woe to them if they do not recognize this time of My visitation" (1160).

What Jesus says isn't meant to frighten but only to shake us awake from sleep and realize that we need to run to him. When God says, "All you who are thirsty, come to the water!" (Isa. 5:1). He means all, not just some. How many will take him up on his invitation?

MAKING SENSE OF CHAOS

"I thought God was a God of mercy, not one who would send tor-ment and trials on his people." Phrased another way, why do bad things happen to good people? Recently, I've had that discussion with several people. I'm no expert and have no way of definitively answering this question; I can only put forth my own opinion and what helps me make sense out of the world.

Above all, God is our Father and created us because he loves us. He did not intend to create a world full of sin; that was the devil's doing. "Therefore, just as through one person sin entered the world, and through sin, death, and thus death came to all, inasmuch as all sinned" (Rom. 5:12). Adam sinned and we feel the effects of that sin to this very day. Consider sin in the light of chaos theory (a butterfly flapping its wings in New York City causes hurricanes in China). One sin by one man thousands of years ago, and now look where we are today: rampant sin everywhere we look. The cycle goes on and on. Someone receives a hurt and repays the hurt with revenge and violence. That's what the devil feeds on and is strengthened by. If we could see the spiritual effects of our sin, we'd recoil in horror. Who's to say that the devil can't take the effects of our individual sin (our agreeing to let more evil into the world) in our neighborhood and use it to kill a little girl halfway around the globe? But God has given us hope in Jesus. Jesus took all the hurt, anger, and pain aimed at him and didn't give any of it back. He broke the cycle with forgive-ness, and out of Jesus came love, healing and mercy. "So through one righteous act acquittal and life came to all" (Rom. 5:18). Just as sin spread to all men, so too can healing and forgiveness if we allow it. The spiritual effects spread in the same way. God can take the merits of our sacrifices and kindness and use them to keep a child from starving. We may never see the good that can come from our fasting and such, but God uses everything we do for the conversion of souls. It's what having faith is about, and it's why forgiveness is so necessary to breaking the cycle of sin.

So there's really no sense in blaming God for the wars, famine, disease and other things that go wrong. They come from what we have done, not from God. When bad things happen, it's because sin affects everyone, not just the sinner. Thank heavens the grace of Jesus's sacrifice is open to everyone as well. All God desires is our conversion. If we allow them, the trials and misfortunes can bring us closer to him by purifying our hearts and making them a fitting throne room. Sin is in the world; we can't help that. Jesus said "In the world you will have trouble, but take courage, I have conquered the world" (John 16:33), and in him we would find peace.

> The light shines in the darkness, and the darkness
> has not overcome it.
>
> —John 1:5

When Jesus said I forgive

Forgiving someone is a hard thing. It can't be done without prayer as a foundation. Our souls are weak and can do nothing on their own. Every good thing comes from God, and this includes the strength to do what we ourselves cannot. If the thought of forgiving someone is troubling, take up the rosary and pray intently the third Luminous Mystery: the proclamation of the kingdom of God with the call to conversion. In this mystery, Jesus proclaims, "Forgiveness of sins for all who draw near to him in humble trust…the inauguration of that ministry of mercy which he continues to exercise until the end of the world, particularly through the Sacrament of Reconciliation which he has entrusted to his Church" (John Paul II, sec. 22).

Through contemplating the Rosary, we can understand the grace of his mercy and allow it to act in our lives. Only through the gift of this mercy can we learn to be gentle with others and ourselves.

When Jesus was dying on the cross, he said, "Father, forgive them, they know not what they do" (Luke 23:34). Oh, how easily we read those words! Yet what did it take for Jesus to utter them? He didn't say them simply to give us an example. Even he, in his human and divine heart, had to mean them too. We can imagine Jesus directed that desire to the soldiers who nailed him to the cross and to the Jewish council who condemned him. Even harder to do, perhaps, was directing that forgiveness toward his apostles who abandoned him, toward Peter who denied him, and even to Judas, who betrayed him. It's one thing to forgive a stranger who knows not what he does, but another thing to forgive family and friends who may know what they are doing. Sometimes it's only by the grace of God that we are able to forgive when the other person denies doing anything wrong at all. In that case, gather up the dignity we have as God's children, trudge through the mud of crushed feelings, and by sheer determination, say in our hearts, "I will forgive you, and I will praise God." Then by the grace of God, that forgiveness will come though we may not feel it for months or longer. Jesus never said it would be easy, but forgiveness is definitely worth it.

Mother's Day

Though not part of the liturgical year, Mother's Day has found a place in the heart of Christians who love and honor the mother of Jesus, the Blessed Virgin Mary. May is filled with the crowning of the Virgin Mary by school children and recitations of the Rosary, the prayer which looks at Jesus through his mother's eyes. How often through the centuries has Mary been the comfort of those without hope, who feel that the world, perhaps even God, has turned against them? In all her beauty, purity, and holiness, this august queen is still approachable because she's fully human like us in all things but sin, a simple peasant girl who said yes to God.

In the silence between Jesus's death and resurrection, perhaps Mary pondered Jesus's last words to her, "'Woman, behold, your son'; Then he said to the disciple, 'Behold, your mother'" (John 19: 26–27). As she'd held the body of her son on the blood-soaked ground, did she recognize the birthing pangs of her spiritual motherhood? Perhaps she at last began to glimpse more of God's plan for her. For some reason, God, who can fill all roles, deemed it necessary that the human race should have not just the triune God but a mother as well. As God gifted Mary with motherhood, may we be given the sense of truly being Mary's children in order to love her with the heart of a child. Then folded within her Immaculate Heart, we can love God in beauty and holiness, pleasing in his sight.

A MOTHER'S PRAYER

Over the years since I've had two children, I've come to appreciate a good many things. Ordinary things like eating a meal undisturbed or finishing a cup of coffee while it's hot are a rarity. Finishing a book? What's that? I used to say three rosaries a day; now I'm lucky to get in one. Prayer changes with time and events, and prayer took on a new light with the attacks on America and the war on terrorism, but mainly, it's a family event that really hit home for me.

On Labor Day of 2001, my six-week-old daughter was hospitalized with viral meningitis. At one point, in the emergency room, I was sent out so they could do a spinal tap in a sterile fashion. I stood outside, listening to my daughter's shrieks and unable to do a thing. The only way I got through was to imagine that Jesus and Mary were in there, holding her in their arms. It was then I became convinced there was no more powerful or passionate prayer on earth than that of a mother. I thought of Mary at the foot of the cross and just what was happening to her as a mother. I realized in a new way the ultimate sacrifice she had made with her yes. She had forsaken every last right she had as a mother. Her will was so united with God's will that she couldn't even rage and scream at the soldiers crucifying her son or even be angry at those who had condemned him. Somewhere deep in her soul, she had, with God, willed his crucifixion. In his last dying breath, she couldn't even hold her son. In a dark world, at that moment, she stood as a shining host at his cross, sacrificing her very being as mother and adoring him whom she loved. The prayer that she sent to heaven at that moment can never be matched, and I was very glad to have her praying with me as I stood in that emergency room, unable to hold my baby. It seems this situation may be applied to a great many people today. Not only to the people who lost their family and friends in the Twin Towers and planes, but to anyone going through any type of sorrow. Jesus gave Mary to us as a mother. What a generous and precious gift! Don't simply put that gift on a shelf and admire it, but use it. Allow yourself to be held in your mother's arms and lean against her as would a child. Let yourself melt a little and feel her strength come through. Mary knows very well that sometimes God's will is hard to understand, but she will help get us through until the day when we can see clearly.

Let us thank God for the gift of Mary. Her role could have ended with Jesus, but Jesus chose to extend her motherhood to all people. Now we have not only our own mothers praying for us, but the mother of Jesus as well. What a powerful intercessor! Any mother who has prayed for her children knows what a fervent prayer that is. Because we are now her children, she prays for us just as passionately. Praise God that Jesus was so generous with his mother, and thank Mary for her prayers for us.

HONORING OUR MOTHER

Since God has firmly established for us a heavenly Mother, a mother who knows and cares for her children and who loves us, guides us, prays for, and cries for us, it's fitting that we get to know her. Personally, I know there is something that swells in my heart when my kids call on me. "Mama, come here!" "Mama, it's dark. Come with me!" "Mama, help me with this!" etc., etc. Even in those times when the persistent calls become irritating (I've not as much patience as our Lady!), I delight in having them call me Mama and putting so much trust in me. Imagine how much more delight Mary has. Yes, it gives her honor to pay her homage as queen, but it is love that is desired. What father wouldn't want his children to love their mother? After all, there is no greater gift in heaven or on earth than love. It may sound funny, but recently, I've caught myself every so often referring to Mary as Mama in my prayers. I was surprised at first when it slipped out, but it sounded so natural. For me, Mary is the one who has led me on the way to Jesus from my earliest school days. It seems only natural to build a relationship with her. After all, Jesus himself refers to his Father as Abba, or Daddy, and invites us to do so as well. Would it be so wrong to love his mother as Jesus did? And we have to admit the way we refer to a person eventually affects our relationship with them. Hopefully, this one will make us grow closer.

On Mother's Day this year, let's remember our own mothers and how they cared, or care, for us. Maybe they were superb at supplying all the material necessities, or maybe circumstances were otherwise. But at heart was probably the anxiousness and desire for us to grow up safe, to be good and live life well. Our Mother Mary wants nothing less. Perhaps our gift to our two mothers can simply be to tell them, "Thank you, Mama. I love you."

IN OUR MOTHER'S ARMS

> Am I not here, I, who am your mother?...Are you not in the hollow of my mantle, in the crossing of my arms? Do you need something more?"
>
> —Our Lady of Guadalupe

I love so many things about being a mom; I can't even begin to list them. One is the almost constant free entertainment my girls provide. I'm fortunate. Their antics and giggles far outweigh their arguments. Other times, I realize God's presence through my kids. My favorite time is during the early morning when I pray the Rosary. Usually, I'll get most of the way through when one daughter will wake and come curl up on my lap silently. Sometimes, I'll finish quietly, or other times, I'll talk to her about our Father. It struck me one day that, spiritually, I do the exact same thing as my daughter. I wake up in the morning, come out to the living room, and curl up in the arms of my mother, the Virgin Mary, as I pray the Rosary. In prayer, she'll tell me about her son. She'll tell me the things one can learn only on their knees, and I'll whisper to her what's in my heart. As I rest in her arms, I know these are the same arms that held the baby Jesus and raised him. She held him in her lap, as I do my girls, and taught him to pray. What did she tell him of his Father in heaven? And finally, those are the same arms that rocked our Lord when he was taken down from the cross. Oh, what we can learn from our mother! How intimately we can know our Lord's passion through his mother's heart! What a gift he has given us!

As a mother, my prayer is that my girls will know God: Father, Son, and Holy Spirit. I can give them all the prayers, instructions, etc., but I can't force the love that comes from knowing him. Our mother Mary desires the same for us as well. She wants us to know him, to speak heart to heart with him in all intimacy, to pray until prayer becomes a joy for us as it is for her. Today let's come away from the world a little, curl up in our mother's arms, and allow her to teach us.

What's in a Name

Ever since I was little, I've always wondered about names and their meanings, whether someone's name reflects their personality or other traits. I read once that one of the visionaries in Medjugorje (where alleged apparitions are occurring) said that God inspires the name parents give to their children. One name which fascinates me is *Mary*.

One thought is that Mary is derived from the Egyptian *mery*, *meryt*, meaning "cherished" or "beloved," certainly fitting for the Blessed Virgin. The Oriental word *mara* means "well-nourished." As

Orientals associate the idea of being well-nourished with perfection in body, they could derive a name from *mara* meaning "beautiful one" or "perfect one." But why would her parents choose an Egyptian or Oriental name? A more popular hypothesis is that Mary is a combination of two Hebrew words *mar* (bitter) and *yam* (sea). Put together into a simple word *maryam*, it renders "bitter one" or "great sorrow."

So what does this mean for us, if anything? We know the life of the Virgin Mary was anything but easy. We only see a fraction of the joys and sorrows of her life. Her shared agony in Jesus's crucifixion easily earns her the title of bitter one or great sorrow. Consider also the love that Jesus preached and the behavior toward our neighbors He encouraged. "Offer no resistance to one who is evil. When someone strikes you on [your] right cheek, turn the other one to him as well" (Matt. 5:39); "love your enemies, and pray for those who persecute you" (Matt. 5:44); "do not blow a trumpet...to win the praise of others" (Matt. 6:2); and "And your Father who sees what is hidden will repay you" (Matt 6:18). Mary, who practiced these words to perfection, models for us the way to live them and is, herself, the example of how our Father will repay us. Love is not easy. Love hurts. How many times do we find ourselves biting our tongue so as not to say that bit of gossip or not to make a stinging reply? I'm sure Mary did all those things too. How often did she not complain about being bone tired only to face piles of laundry or cooking and think to herself that no one notices? Those bitten-off responses, complaints left unspoken, every encounter with neighbors that left them facing God's joy at our expense could have sown in us seeds of bitterness. It's in our nature to want to show off to others what we've done, to blow the horn, so to speak. Yet rather than letting bitterness take root and turn cancerous (as we so often do), Mary turned it over to the Father, and he replaced it with peace and strength to endure. We must do the same and not let our hidden sacrifices turn ugly, but ask the Holy Spirit to fill us with sweet joy and love great enough to desire to follow Jesus and his cross. Just as Mary's reward was being crowned Queen of Heaven, the beauty of our heavenly crown will reflect our lives on earth and all the things that only our Father saw. Give us patience to see that crown! Blessed Mary, our human mother full of grace, pray for us!

✦ ✦ ✦

PENTECOST

Now here she was again with Jesus and the other apostles. "I am with you always," he said as they walked up the hill, "until the end of the age" (Matt. 28:20). Miraculously, before them, he began his ascent to heaven. Jesus looked into his mother's eyes, and then he was gone. Mary's heart constricted. She had lost him again. Jesus, her son, had gone back to his Father in heaven. Perhaps she was no longer needed...

So it may have seemed. Mary went back with the other apostles to the upper room and prayed and waited. Jesus had promised them the Holy Spirit, but they didn't know what that meant. For now, perhaps, Mary dealt with the joy of the resurrection and the emptiness after the ascension, once more pondering all these things in her heart. Her son was gone. What was she supposed to do now? Then nine days later came the gift. The Holy Spirit rushed into their lives as flames of fire, filling their hearts with joy and understanding. Perhaps with the birthday of the church and the three thousand added in one day, Mary began to see the scope of her role as spiritual mother. She would guide the newly baptized in the way of her son Jesus, the Son of God. She could tell them as she once said so long ago, "Do whatever he tells you" (John 2:5). She would show them how to love him as she does and live entirely for God, making their lives beautiful offerings for him until some day they would be together in heaven. Yes, this was her mission; she could feel the certainty in her heart. "O Father," Mary prayed in earnest. "Let me bring them all to you, all of them everywhere! Help me teach everyone to say yes to you!"

THE SPIRIT AND THE BRIDE

Speaking of Mary without speaking of the Holy Spirit is impossible since, by the conception of Jesus, they are espoused. During the Easter season, we prepare for the coming of the Holy Spirit at Pentecost, the foundation of the church. In the chapter 21 of Revelation, the bride of the Lamb is depicted as the new Jerusalem, the church in glory. Mary is the embodiment of the church; she is also the bride of the Lamb. There is no better way to come to know the Holy Spirit than to know Mary, his spouse. Likewise, the more the Holy Spirit finds Mary in our hearts, the more delighted he is to come and dwell in us as well.

The Spirit is perhaps the least understood of the persons of the Trinity. Maybe it's because the terms used to describe him are rather vague: a wind, a fire. Simply put, the Spirit is the love which flows between the Father and the Son in a constant communion. The gift that Jesus gave the first Pentecost in the Holy Spirit coming to us was the ability for us to share that superhuman love of the Father and Son with each other. To spread and continue the church that Jesus was asking for was beyond our human capabilities. We simply would not have the strength. So Jesus gave us his own love, faith, and endurance, his own hope that we would be united with him through his gospel. Mary was with the apostles when the Spirit came, yet nowhere is mentioned the role she took in the continuation of the church. Did she go out preaching or was she a quiet pillar of strength and prayer for the apostles? Whichever it was, we may still learn how to recognize the Spirit in our lives through an examination of some of her virtues.

The virtues of the Holy Spirit and Mary's virtues are these: faith, hope, charity, humility, patience, perseverance, and obedience. There are examples of all these in the gospels, from Mary's obedience and humility in saying yes to the Father, her charity in visiting Elizabeth, to her perseverance in standing beneath Jesus's cross. She is the perfect model for us in all these things. If we try to imitate and love Mary, the Spirit will take delight in finding another lover of his spouse and wrap our hearts with his presence. Therefore, since everything of Mary is directed toward Jesus, we will also come to love him. Our human hearts alone are incapable of such a love worthy of God, so it's through the grace of the Spirit that we're able to fix our gaze longingly on him.

The Spirit can't touch our lives without us feeling the results. Yes, there is hardship in living a virtuous life. We're not given patience without the opportunity to practice it! But there are fruits of the Spirit to be enjoyed as well: charity, peace, joy and patience, kindness, goodness, long-suffering and meekness, faith, moderation, continence, and chastity. There are also other gifts, such as the charismatic ones the apostles discovered right away and all that are intended to build up God's kingdom and bring others closer to him.

There is an outpouring of the Holy Spirit today unlike any since the first Pentecost. This Spirit is the first of two awesome gifts Jesus has given to help us on our journey to the Father, the other being his mother, Mary. Let's listen and learn from them carefully. They'll never contradict each other as both have the same message seen in Revelation: "The Spirit and the bride say, 'Come'" (Rev. 22:17).

REJUVENATION

Renew your wonders this day as by a new Pentecost.

—Pope St. John XXIII
praying for the Vatican Council

Have you ever read the Bible, specifically the New Testament letters, and noticed something radically different between the early Christian communities and our churches today? Perhaps a certain vibrancy, a sure faith that God will take an active part in their lives, and he did? Today in most communities we live out the commandments of God and try our best to be good Christians, but we're lacking that energy. That energy is the Holy Spirit. How did we lose sight of the third part of the Trinity, and how do we get it back?

In the beginning of the church, God poured out his spirit because it's what he promised (Luke 24:49, Acts 1:8, 2:38–39), and such an outpouring was needed to help raise up believers. People, upon hearing about Jesus, were baptized and then the apostles laid hands on them, and they received the Holy Spirit. It was something that was expected to happen. Wonders and miracles were worked to build up the body of believers. However, by the fourth century, the manifestations of the Holy Spirit were much less frequent; and by the early twentieth century, the concept of Holy Spirit hardly mentioned by Catholics at all. So what brought on the change? My personal opinion is that the devil is harder at work in this century than ever to make the church lose her way. If we are ever to guide the world back to Christ, it will take more than human power; the Holy Spirit has to intervene. In the Catholic Church, this happened definitively with the charismatic renewal after Vatican II. Today, there is an outpouring of the spiritual gifts similar to New Testament times. Yes, we've always had the Spirit in baptism and confirmation, now it's just being stirred up in us. Some might say, "Oh, those gifts aren't for me," or "I don't need those." But the Bible and church teach us to expect those gifts and use them in whatever ministry we have. The Decree on the Apostolate of the Laity states,

> For the exercise of this apostolate, the Holy Spirit… gives the faithful special gifts also (cf. 1 Cor.12:7), "allotting them to everyone according as He wills" (1 Cor. 12:11)…From the acceptance of these charisms, including those which are more elementary, there arise for each believer the right and duty to use them in the church and in the world for the good of men and the building up of the church. (Paul VI, sec. 3)

In Mark 16:14ff, Jesus tells us that everyone who believes in him will be able to do wonderful things.

Jesus is telling us to ask and not to be afraid. He wants to give us these gifts; it's what he intended. He wants us to help each other on our journey to him. What's the effect of the Holy Spirit? It's like hearing about someone for a long time and knowing them well second hand. Then one day you meet them face to face and fall in love. It's that experience, that change in our relationship with Christ, which will energize and guide our witnessing Christ. May we ask the Blessed Virgin Mary, who is spouse to the Holy Spirit, to help us be open to the gifts of the Spirit just as she was in that upper room on the first Pentecost.

Jesus's second mission

A couple of weeks ago, I had the wonderful opportunity of hearing the Preacher to the Papal Household, Fr. Raniero Cantalamessa, speak at a conference. He is a Franciscan Capuchin priest, very mild of manner and humble. He smiled as he said that, by nature, he is not a joyful person, and I have to differ. When he speaks of God, his face lights up and there is such enthusiasm in his voice. One can almost see the love he has for Christ radiating from him. He spoke passionately about the need for the Holy Spirit. Let me share some of these things.

Father Cantalamessa spoke of Jesus's second mission. (Jesus's first mission, which is mentioned in all four gospels, is to redeem us from sin by his death on the cross.) His second mission, also mentioned in all four gospels, is to give us the Holy Spirit. John the Baptist continually preached that he baptized with water, but that one would come who would baptize with the Holy Spirit. John saw the Holy Spirit descend on Jesus after his baptism. Unlike in Old Testament times when the Spirit gave a message and left, the Spirit stayed with Jesus. After Jesus's resurrection, he gave that same Spirit to us, telling us that whoever is baptized could be saved and be able to do wonderful things. Pope St. John Paul II encouraged us to bring to life the culture of Pentecost. The Pope has stated, "Yes! The Renewal in the Spirit can be considered a special gift of the Spirit to the church in our time...In a special way continue to love and spread love for the *prayer of praise*, the form of prayer that recognizes more immediately that God is God" (John Paul II 2002, sec. 2 and 4).

In *Novo millennio ineunte*, we are told that ours is the wonderful and demanding task to become reflections of the light of Christ (sec. 54). Father Cantalamessa says to look at John 17. The love the Father has for Jesus and Jesus's love for the Father are so tangible their embodiment is the Holy Spirit. When we love Jesus with the love of the Father, then we share in the Holy Spirit and are one with them.

Anyone can be baptized in the Spirit; we don't have to be saints. Father Cantalamessa thought he didn't need it; he was already a priest for several years and was doing just fine. But a few days after he was baptized in the Spirit, he sat down and opened his breviary as always and began to read the Psalms. Whoa, where did these psalms come from? It was like they were written just for him. Why hadn't he ever read these before? It was one of four signs the baptism *took*: the scriptures come alive, an increased love for prayer, a desire to praise and pray with God's people, and a desire to evangelize. Other charisms will accompany these. In John 14:15ff, Jesus describes the Holy Spirit. He and the Father intend it as a gift, one who will help us and always be with us. We needn't be worried or afraid. In Luke 11:11–13, Jesus says that the Father will give us only good things. He wants to give the Holy Spirit to anyone who asks.

SETTING THE WORLD ABLAZE

> Proclamation of the Gospel must be for us…a primary and unavoidable duty.

> —Pope Benedict XVI

No matter where you travel today, you can probably find Christians most anywhere, either in the open or in hiding, but they're there. Twelve men did that. Twelve apostles of Jesus Christ converted us all. I pray the passion that filled their hearts inspires us as well as we continue our mission in the new evangelization.

Our mission is as old as the church itself, ever since Jesus said to go out and preach the Gospel to all nations. There are churches on practically every corner, so we should all be converted and living our lives fully for God, right? Then what happened? Did the prince of darkness worm his way into our lives and allure us with worldly attractions, and did we become overwhelmed with the anxieties of the day? Pretty much. The devil's doing a good job, so it's up to us to do ours better. If our neighbors have grown cold, then it's up to us to rekindle that spark. In Pope Benedict XVI's address for World Mission Day in 2009, he said that "At stake is the eternal salvation of persons, the goal and the fulfillment of human history and universe." St. John Paul II aimed the new evangelization at fallen-away Catholics or Catholics in name only who didn't really know Jesus, but he later revised it to include all people. It's rather unlikely, in our circles, that we know anyone who's never heard the name of Jesus. Many people shy away when we try to speak to them about God like they're having an allergic reaction, or they simply tune out any mention of him. Most people don't go for being preached at and given a list of dos and don'ts; maybe that's happened to them before. We can have all the education and methods at our disposal, but that won't necessarily change hearts. Pope Paul VI wrote in *Evangelii nuntiandi*, "Techniques of evangelization are good, but even the most advanced ones could not replace the gentle action of the Spirit. The most perfect preparation of the evangelizer has no effect without the Holy Spirit. Without the Holy Spirit the most convincing dialectic has no power over the heart of man." (75)

The twelve apostles certainly had no training, but they had spent three years with Jesus, learning from him, and they had the power of the Spirit on their side. All they did was talk to people. They shared what Jesus had done for them in their lives, and their enthusiasm was contagious. Now we must ask ourselves, Are we that enthusiastic? Are we so excited about what Jesus has done for us that we speak about him contagiously? If not, then we need to become that excited. Ask the Holy Spirit for help, and then pray, pray, pray. We must be fertile ground first in order to accept all the graces God showers on us or grace will run off, unable to penetrate our dry, hardened souls. Those graces, that prayer for ourselves and others will help others to be more receptive to God working in their hearts so that someday they will be ready for him. We can preach all we want, but without prayer and the Holy Spirit, hearts will not be converted. The world's grown cold. Will we let him use us to set the world ablaze again?

OUTSIDE OUR COMFORT ZONE

As we draw nearer to Pentecost, I imagine a challenge given to us by the Holy Spirit: to follow God and allow him to so work in us that we'll never be the same. How ready are we to answer that call?

Most of us like to think of ourselves as good Catholics or Christians who do what we can to live pleasingly to God, or at

104

least not to mess up enormously. But how far are we willing to go to advance his cause? We're pretty comfortable going to church on Sundays, saying grace before meals or even bedtime prayers. We manage to keep God in his compartment in our lives, and we're okay with that because it's safe; it's what we expect. But what if he started to leak out? Would we allow the name of Jesus to pass our lips (not in swearing) even though we knew the instant it did, we'd be labeled as religious freaks? Quite often when God works, it's not in huge miracles (although he can and does) but in quiet, personal interaction using each other. Can we allow him in our personal space? What if we're feeling anxious and could use some prayers? Rather than putting ourselves on a distant prayer line, could we pray one on one? Not too many Catholics are comfortable asking people to pray with them, yet Jesus said, "If two of you agree on earth about anything for which they are to pray, it shall be granted to them by my heavenly Father" (Matt. 18:19). Honestly, if someone were to ask if they could pray with you, what would your reaction be? Jesus so wants to be in our hearts. He wants us to be comfortable with him. He will never force us, but he will challenge us. Sometimes he will work outside our comfort zone, but he is still God. He will wait for us to come to Him, and when He sees our hearts are ready He will start to give us his gifts. The Holy Spirit is the promised gift of the Father, but he is also God himself. When we see the Holy Spirit working in ways our minds can't explain, we can't just deny it's him or say, "That's too weird for me." Could we be challenged and open our hearts to say, maybe this is God too? Remember, "my thoughts are not your thoughts, nor are your ways my ways" (Isa. 55:8).

Think about it as we pray for the Holy Spirit to come this Pentecost. Will we allow him to change us, work in us, and use us as he wishes to bring others to him?

THE GIVING OF GIFTS

I would like to share something I saw in prayer at a charismatic conference a few weeks ago. Just for an instant, an image popped into my mind of Jesus holding a large bucket on his right side and pouring from it all sorts of graces, blessings, and gifts. They were flowing out like a river onto the people. Jesus was not only smiling but laughing. Then it was gone. My only thought was that I had imagined it on my own because why would Jesus be laughing so hard? However, not two minutes later, a woman went up to the podium and described in detail the exact same image I'd seen. Talk about confirmation! We agreed that Jesus was laughing so hard because, one, he loves giving us graces; and two, (and this is what tickled him so much) because we were openly receiving them. We wanted his gifts.

So to ask a general question, Why does God bother with giving us gifts at all? The simplest of all reasons is that he is our Father and he loves us. When we love someone, we give them a gift as a sign of our love, and doesn't it make us feel special when we receive a gift? Ah, but that's too easy, you say. Nothing's free these days. What's the catch? The beauty of these gifts is that they are free; we haven't done anything to earn them. God gives them to us gratis. All He wants is our gratitude and our love. "I desire mercy, not sacrifice" (Matt. 12:7).

What are some of the gifts God gives us? There are more than the basic seven gifts we learn about in confirmation from Isaiah 11:2: wisdom, piety, fortitude, fear of the Lord, counsel, understanding, and knowledge. There are also the fruits of the Spirit mentioned in Galatians 5:22–23: love, joy, peace, patience, kindness, self-control, generosity, faithfulness, gentleness and modesty. These two sets of gifts are important for our own holiness. They are built up in our mannerisms, in how we love one another and react to others. The last of the gifts are charismatic gifts that Paul mentions throughout his letters. Some of these are tongues, interpretation of tongues, prophecy, words of wisdom, knowledge and revelation, faith, healing, miracles, etc. (1 Cor. 12:8–10). Charismatic gifts are for building up the community, the church. They are supposed to catch people's attention, to get them to say, "What? How did that happen? Tell me more." They become one way of evangelizing. Yes, there are right and wrong ways to use the gifts. Paul very clearly states dos and don'ts in Corinthians 14. For example, in a charismatic prayer group, we speak in tongues as our direct prayer to God. We have interpretation and prophecy. We understand what's going on. But a stranger would think we were crazy. It would be better to speak a word of prophecy or revelation in plain language so someone could understand and be drawn to God. But all are meant to be alluring, to bring people to our Father.

God—Father, Son, and Spirit—wants to take an active part in our lives. We know the Father and Son. Let's not squelch the Spirit, who wants to shower down his love and gifts on us as well.

ARE WE TO UNDERSTAND?

My six-year-old daughter came up to me after her first soccer practice and wondered if she'd seen her doctor on the sidelines. I said that yes, her son was one of her teammates now.

"But," she said, "she's my doctor."

"Yes, she is," I'd replied. "But she has a little boy just like I have you."

My daughter put her hands on her hips and cocked her head to one side. "How am I supposed to understand this?" I love how little minds work.

How much of that reflects our attitude toward God in some matters? We would love to understand the world and everything he does. We want to know the whys and why nots. And then, when something happens that's beyond our comprehension, we put our hands on our hips and ask God, "How am I supposed to understand this?" Sometimes we ask in defiance. We say that unless we understand—unless he gives us a good reason for it—we will not believe in God anymore. How our Father must shake his head at us as we shake ours at our children, partially amused, knowing we can never explain the world to them entirely. Perhaps his response to us is, "For my thoughts are not your thoughts, nor are your ways my ways, says the Lord. As high as the heavens are above the earth, so high are my ways above your ways and my thoughts above your thoughts" (Isa. 55:8–9). Just as our children must accept "because that's the way things are" from us, we may need to accept that response from our Father. The world will never understand God, and we cannot reason our way to faith.

We don't settle that easily though. We still want to know why God is the way he is and does things the way he does. Yet the best way to understand someone is to get to know them. Jesus said that anyone who has seen him has seen the Father. Therefore, we must know Jesus. Jesus didn't tell us, "I know the way to heaven," he said, "I am the way" (John 14:6). Jesus said he would send us a helper, the Paraclete, the Spirit of Truth, who would instruct us in everything and guide us to all truth. Isn't that what we are just dying to know, the truth? No one knows the Father and the Son better than the Spirit, who is completely obedient. We need to surrender all to the Spirit. Those would be the optimal words here,—surrender and obedience. If we surrender to the Spirit and try with all our heart to obey our Father's will, what could be more pleasing to God? What could be more beautiful than to say, "Jesus, I trust in you," and humbly submitting our wills to his with childlike faith that he will take care of us? He has supplied everything for us down to our next meal. Need we worry? He will continue to take care of us. We may or may not ever understand, but we can love and trust and learn to live that in our lives. How radically our lives would change if that happened!

Most High God, Father, Son and Spirit, I surrender!

Jesus, I trust in you!

DRAWING PEOPLE IN

"Let us implore from God the grace of a new Pentecost for the church in America. May tongues of fire, combining burning love of God and neighbor with zeal for the spread of Christ's Kingdom, descend on all present!" (Benedict XVI 2008).

Do we really mean what we pray for? "Come, Holy Spirit, fill the hearts of your faithful and kindle in them the fire of your love. Send forth your Spirit and they shall be created, and You shall renew the face of the earth" (Priests of the Sacred Heart, n.d.).

Have we stopped to think about what that prayer means? It's a prayer of anticipation and hope, one of expecting God to fill us with his Spirit. It is also a prayer that God in his mercy is fulfilling today as he is pouring out his Spirit on all humanity. When Pope St. John Paul II was speaking to various groups representing the church in 2004, he said, "Thanks to the Charismatic Movement, a multitude of Christians…have rediscovered Pentecost as a living reality in their daily lives. I hope that the *spirituality of Pentecost* will spread in the Church." Someimes the passion of praise breaks out, and we lift our hand in worship, in awe and in wonder of God. Such expressiveness, or enthusiasm, in prayer can often be viewed suspiciously. Often it seems among us Catholics that our masses are scripted—when to stand, kneel, or sit—as if our moving around would mess up God's head count! But that's where the mass is different from a prayer service where we are free to move around as we wish.

The Holy Mass is beyond our comprehension as a solemn (yet joyful) celebration of the sacrifice of Jesus. It is a mystery of God's love manifest here on earth. Unless the priest is aware of and invites these expressions at Mass, it's best not to inundate people with them and possibly be disruptive. This is where that hesitancy in others I mentioned earlier comes in. People see things they're unfamiliar with and shy away, and we are suddenly branded as fanatical charismatics. Anyone baptized in the Spirit needs to ease other people into the Spirit-filled life. "Zeal for your house consumes me" (Ps. 69:10). True, but there's a time and place to exhibit that zeal. One of the main fruits of baptism in the Spirit is the desire to witness for Jesus. "Stir into flame the gift of God…God did not give us a spirit of cowardice, but rather of power and love and self-control" (2 Tim. 1:6–7). God doesn't want to scare people off but to draw them in through love, faith, and common sense. Then they'll hunger and thirst for more of him, and we can all truly pray with our hearts, "Come, Holy Spirit, fill the hearts of Your faithful."

BREAKING OUR MOLDS

Go, therefore, and make disciples of all nations.

—Matthew 28:19

"It was easier because they didn't know me." That was what my friend said, referring to her missionary time in Russia. It's so much easier to witness to people who are vaguely familiar with Christ and who don't know you personally than to share Christ with your next door neighbor. So why is that? "Because they won't laugh at you, and if they do, it doesn't hurt as much. People back home have expectations of how you're supposed to behave. You live with them. They've seen you grow. So now to break out of a mold and be called a holy roller. Well, it's not easy."

It's food for thought, isn't it? The last thing Jesus told us was to go and teach everyone what he commanded us. How often do we actually do that? Maybe it is easier to go off to Russia for a while. We both agreed that it takes guts to preach (by example or word) to those in our backyard. I find that, for myself, I still take the easy way. I talk about God when I go to church or among my group of Christian friends. But they already know God and honor him. How much harder it is to go to our workplaces or neighbors where perhaps it's "politically incorrect" to speak about God, and we think it's too risky. There are appropriate times and places to speak, and we need to recognize and take advantage of those times. So then, what if we're just too nervous and say, this isn't for me etc.? The apostles were nervous. Perhaps downright scared. But Jesus had told them "Do not worry about how you are to speak or what you are to say...it will not be you who speak but the Spirit of your Father speaking through you" (Matt. 10:19–20). It is no different for us. The exact same Spirit will speak through us. Yes, it's the same Spirit we were given in baptism and reaffirmed in confirmation. Baptism wasn't just an entrance rite into a club. God's own Spirit was given to us and equipped us to become his children with a share in grace and responsibility. At our confirmation, we trained in the knowledge of the gifts so that, like a soldier training for battle, we would know our resources from which to draw and live for Christ. Contrary to some opinion, confirmation shouldn't be the end of our religious education but a new beginning. We need to know our faith well in order to do battle in a culture of death. How can we convert others if we haven't fanned into flame a passion for God in our own hearts? Let's be like children at Christmas exploring their gifts. Let's explore what our Father has offered to us in the Holy Spirit. If this Holy Spirit is going to speak through us, then we need to know all about him. If he will give us the guts to shout from the mountaintops, proclaiming what God has done for us, then so be it. Don't we all need to be stirred up a little out of our complacency sometimes? We're not going to speak about God unless we want to. The Holy Spirit will give us that desire.

COURAGE TO FACE THE WORLD

I came in a roundabout way to pondering the second half of John, chapter 15. It started out with Pentecost and the wonderful coming of the Holy Spirit. Jesus knew that as much as the disciples might like to have him stay with them, it would be better to have the Holy Spirit come and be with everyone. This way, everyone, from least to greatest, could have access to God. The world would be forever changed now that Jesus had come. The Son revealed the Father and the Father's plan of gathering us all to himself in heaven. He revealed the Father's desire that we would all be one in his heart. Now, did people accept that plan? Some did, but most didn't, and they crucified Jesus for it. They couldn't bear the thought that God could be Father, and yet Jesus only spoke the truth. We will also speak the truth as prompted by the Spirit. So the Spirit not only helps us become witnesses of the Father, but it also sustains us. It gives us the sometimes supernatural strength necessary to endure whatever people will throw at us.

In John 15:18, Jesus says, "If the world hates you, realize that it hated me first." He's pretty blunt when he points out that people will respect us as much as they respected him. This is the price we must pay for being his followers. And yet, because we love our Lord and our Father in heaven, because we so desire other people to know the joy that comes from loving him, we willingly step on the road to Calvary. When we say we resemble our Father, we share not only in his glory but also the suffering that accompanies it. We will resemble Jesus in the wounds he received, not only from enemies but from friends, and those wounds hurt the deepest. We can expect no less.

People will think our behavior crazy, but we must keep in mind that the world does not understand the folly of the cross because it doesn't know the Father. Perhaps Jesus will use the sufferings of ours to help bring about their conversion.

Jesus didn't forewarn us that we would be hated and then leave us with no help. He said, "Take courage, I have conquered the world" (John 16:33). He told us we would receive power when the promise of the Father, the Holy Spirit, would come upon us. What a promise! The many gifts, fruits, and graces of the Holy Spirit are too numerous to count. There are the traditional Isaiah gifts we learn about when we're confirmed; all the charismatic gifts mentioned in Corinthians; the fruits listed in Galatians, chapter 5; the armor in Ephesians, chapter 6; and more than we can imagine. What an awesome gift! Let us pray for a fresh outpouring of the Spirit to make us effective witnesses and to give us the courage to bear the marks of his divine image. Praised be the Holy Trinity!

ORDINARY TIME II

CORPUS CHRISTI

After Pentecost, the longest section of Ordinary Time begins, again what I like to call the peanut-butter-and-jelly days. Few major feast days are celebrated during these months. For the most part nothing spectacular happens, just the days that sustain us and fill most of our life. Perhaps a calmer season is what we need to ponder all that's happened: the Last Supper, Jesus's death and resurrection, his teaching about his being the bread of life, then Pentecost and the Holy Spirit empowering us to fulfill our mission to go and baptize all the world. It's a lot to take in. Maybe that's why the church gives us the feast of the Body and Blood of Christ (Corpus Christi) at the start of these days. The institution of the Eucharist is rightfully celebrated on Holy Thursday when Jesus proclaimed at the Last Supper the bread and wine was his body and blood. However, the overwhelming events of the following days—Jesus's death and resurrection—often overshadow the first. Now, fourteen days after Pentecost, we have time to consider the miracle of what the blessed Trinity has done for us without the immediate sadness of Jesus's passion. Some of the Mass readings for summer help us to ponder the Eucharist by focusing on the sixth chapter of John, Jesus's bread of life discourse. We can't easily dismiss Jesus's words as only symbolic. He didn't die a symbolic death; the crucifixion was quite real. Just because we don't understand fully how or why God would work in such a manner, doesn't mean he can't or won't. Admittedly, "What eye has not seen, and ear has not heard, and what has not entered the human heart, what God has prepared for those who love him" (1 Cor. 2:9). This side of death, the closest we'll come to understanding God's love for us is by learning about the Eucharist.

Jesus himself has linked our study of the Eucharist with that of his Sacred Heart, five days after the Body and Blood of Christ comes the feast of the Sacred Heart of Jesus. Devotion to the Heart of Jesus has been around since the soldier put his lance into Jesus's side and blood and water gushed forth. As described by one of the early church fathers, St. Justin Martyr (d. 165) in his *Dialogue*, "We the Christians are the true Israel which springs from Christ, for we are carved out of His heart as from a rock." Although it was celebrated throughout the church, the sacred heart wasn't given its own feast day until the apparitions of Jesus to St. Margaret Mary Alacoque (1647–1690). By devoting ourselves to making reparation to a heart so wounded, we grow in love and begin to resemble him. Likewise, devotion to the Immaculate Heart of Mary (whose feast is a day after the Sacred Heart) will help us to love Jesus with the heart of his mother. Honoring Mary doesn't mean we're setting her up as a goddess next to Jesus. We love her because Jesus loved her, and he wants us to imitate him. Everything in Mary's life is aimed toward God; she would never take anything that belonged to him. Mary's heart is entirely God's, and she loves him more perfectly than any of us. So if we imitate Mary, we are learning to love God more perfectly. How can we not take advantage of so great an opportunity?

The Immaculate Heart of Mary

"When the days were completed for their purification according to the law of Moses, they took him up to Jerusalem to present him to the Lord, just as it is written in the law of the Lord, 'Every male that opens the womb shall be consecrated to the Lord,' and to offer the sacrifice of 'a pair of turtledoves or two young pigeons,' in accordance with the dictate in the law of the Lord" (Luke 2:22–24).

The birth of a baby, obeying the law by presenting him to God, how simple it all seems! Yet what a wonderful gift we were given in that ritual.

When Jesus gave Mary to us as mother, he gave us access to her graces as well. By Mosaic law, Mary presented Jesus to God. Because of God's grace, Mary also presents each one of us as her children. Imagine, being presented to God through the Immaculate Heart of

Mary! What a privilege! However, we must ask for this grace. Mary would not intrude on our free will any more than God would. Once we ask Mary to present us to God, we may imagine ourselves in Mary's arms as she stands within the temple. Imagine yourself nestled in the folds of her garment, next to her heart, and she looking at you, joyfully raising you up to be offered to God. Abandon yourself to her doing, and she will gently nurture and mold you as she did the child Jesus. Then through the purity of her heart, she will bring us before our Father in prayer. Our Lady does this each and every day if only we ask her.

If it's hard to imagine being presented to God by Mary, think of it this way: Whenever someone would go before a king, he was always announced by the herald. What if, as you came in the great hall, the herald stood aside and instead of his announcement, the queen herself came off her throne and walked down to your side? She then takes your hand, leads you up to the throne, and presents you to the king. This is exactly what Mary does for us. She does this not because we think we are of some importance, but because God thinks we are so important. What a humbling thought: that God thinks we are important enough to be presented by his own mother.

If we have taken the first step of asking Mary to present us through her Immaculate Heart, then we, by our asking, are obliged to go further. Mary won't do all the work for us; we have to want to be made like her heart as well. The best way to do this is through an act of consecration. By consecrating ourselves to Mary's Immaculate Heart, we are telling God, through Mary, that we want to be like her in everything. In all of our thoughts, words, and actions, we will do whatever Mary wants. How do we know what she wants of us? Quite simply, Mary wants us to "do whatever he tells you" (John 2:5). There are several different forms of consecration, and it doesn't really matter which is made as long as it's made with the heart.

"In our total consecration to Mary, she takes all our thoughts, words, and actions and makes them pleasing to Jesus by *purifying* them in her love, clothing them in her merits, and presenting them to His Eucharistic Heart that He may see and love in us what He sees and loves in His Mother" (Lucia 1984, 19).

Let's take advantage of this beautiful gift Jesus has given us in his mother and offer ourselves to her that she may present us to God.

INSPIRING EACH OTHER

The church year is filled with many events and holidays during fall, winter, and spring to remind us of Jesus, but summer is lacking much to highlight its days. So often it happens that when we go on vacation, we accidentally vacation from God as well. How easy it is to kick back and relax! But now is when we must be extra vigilant because it's so easy to forget what's not right before our eyes. Unlike the ups and downs of our life when we run to God with praise or sorrow, how often, when life is going well, do we forget about him? If we take the time to remember God outside of exciting events and cultivate a relationship with him, then he won't be such a stranger to us when we really need him.

Over the summer, I have had the wonderful opportunity of renewing some old friendships. We try to gather every year, but for some of us, it's more like two or three before we can coordinate our trips. In between, there might be an occasional e-mail, but we're pretty much busy with our lives in our respective locations at opposite coasts. When we meet, watch out! The joy of introducing new families and little ones, catching up on the year's events, and sharing visions of the future swirl in our conversations. Since then, I've been marveling at the ingenuity of God and how he uses our own friends to help us know him better.

We have each come from different walks of life with our own experiences. Over the years, we have all come (or are coming) to know God through various means; some are just beginning their journeys. Yet we all have something to give to each other whether it's the sure faith of having traveled with God for years or the freshness and excitement of just coming to know him. We see how the others see God and add that to our own knowledge and love for him. God knows how limited we are in our perceptions and that we could never contain him, but we can see through someone else's eyes and add their appreciation to our own. Perhaps that is why in Isaiah 6:3, the seraphim cry, "Holy is the Lord" to each other. God knows his own attributes, but with each of us describing our own vision to the other we more fully appreciate the depth and beauty of God.

May we always help each other to know, and bring others closer to knowing, the glory of God!

> Then Francis spoke:
> 'Dear brothers,
> let's thank God
> who wants us to know His wisdom
> even through simple people.
> God gives speech to those who cannot speak;
> God gives wisdom to those who are unlettered.'
> We praise Him. Amen. (Demaray, 1992, 52–53)

I'M WITH YOU ALWAYS

Isn't it funny how some things appear to change over time? During my visit home a few weeks ago, I made several nostalgic stops around town. Places and distances appeared smaller, and people appeared older. What was strangest was going to Chautauqua, a community where I had spent every summer for nineteen years. It is a place so familiar, and while some people knew me, to many, I was a stranger. Considering days gone by was rather like looking at a stream leaving the fountain and going to the sea—that particular patch of water is gone and can't be relived. We can't live in memories. There was one thing though that wasn't a memory. In a small town up the river, I stopped in a church to pay a visit to Jesus. As I stepped in the door, I saw that the Eucharist was on the altar for adoration. I knelt down, looking on the gleaming gold of the monstrance and the thin white sliver of bread within. My heart flooded with knowledge that this was Jesus, the same yesterday, today, and tomorrow. The same Jesus was there as I was growing up and adoring him then, just as I was now. He shared all of my joys and sorrows, my current anxieties, and whatever will come. He never left me. With joy, I knew that Jesus shared in every one of my memories, and he is my constant. He said he would be and has kept that promise. I considered how Jesus has been with me, not only throughout my life but everywhere I've gone as well. I've traveled extensively. We expect to find God in our free country, but I've even found him in the former communist Soviet Union. "My travels and my rest you mark…Where can I hide from your spirit? From your presence, where can I flee?…Even there your hand will guide me, your right hand hold me fast" (Ps. 139:3, 7, 10). God's presence is not only like the air we breathe but also the ground on which we walk. Where can we go to escape the ground? High buildings? Their base is on the ground, and we can't stay indoors forever. Airplanes? What goes up must come down. We can try to escape the ground, and for a while, we may even succeed, but it will always be there to catch us when we fall. Like a magnet drawing us in, God's love calls to our heart. And just like earth's gravity, we can run away from that love. What happens when we break free? Do we wander aimlessly about exploring? As St. Augustine said, "Our hearts are restless until they rest in Thee." In the end, hopefully, we come home. He is always there, waiting for us. He never left. Jesus is keeping his promise. "I am with you always, until the end of the age" (Matt 28:20).

THE STRUGGLE

"But nothing has ever said to me 'God exists,' so why should I?" A friend of mine uttered these words over cups of tea at three in the morning. Several of us had been discussing everything from Plato to particle physics since 10:00 p.m. One friend was just home after spending time abroad in the missions, others were in various states of life and faith. Now I listened as my missionary friend tossed out every quote in the Bible as to why my agnostic friend should believe in God. My nonbelieving friend pointed out that she had spent hours asking these very questions several times in her life, and if she's willing to spend the time asking, why doesn't God just come and tell her, "I exist"? I inwardly smiled at that. Skywriting would be nice, but that belays faith. I suggested that the Holy Spirit was already work-ing in her by giving her the desire to know God. However, beyond a casual curiosity, nothing has ever motivated her to put forth the energy to believe in someone she's not sure exists. How does one go from not believing to realizing there is a higher power out there? She wanted to know why it was so important to us that she believe, or that anyone else other than ourselves believe. We obviously have our faith and that's fine, and she's perfectly content with her life. So why mess with things? I could tell her that my belief in God helps me make sense out of life and suffering, but she's fine with her interpre-tation of life. Why do I desire her belief? How could I explain the joy and freedom that come from loving God?

I found it interesting that she said she's never found a need to believe in a deity, but now her young daughter is starting to ask ques-tions about God. She figured she "ought to find out about him," so she could talk to her daughter. The way she phrased that makes me think she already believes God is out there, she just hasn't acknowl-edged it to herself yet. So now I'll pray that the Holy Spirit will quicken a desire for God in her heart, and that her thirst will begin to be quenched as she drinks in knowledge of him. If God can use me in bringing her around, so be it. Surely, we all know someone like this. Let's allow God to use us to bring them home if only be means of our prayer. This is how he builds his church, one soul at a time. Blessed be God forever.

THE ARMOR OF GOD

I never thought of my tomato plants as wearing armor, but thanks to my six-year-old daughter, I now have that image indelibly imprinted on my mind. As I was putting the cages around my tomatoes, I was telling her about the Ten Commandments and how, like the cages, they would help us grow up straight and bear good fruit. She immediately likened it to a knight in shining armor in that no enemy would get though. Of course, that made me think of all sorts of things.

My thoughts come down to this: If we were to be captured by the enemy (Satan), would he know which side we were on? Do we have on the armor of God? Physically speaking, do we wear any crosses or medals, scapulars; have a rosary in our pockets, anything? Spiritually, do we know the truths taught by the church? Do we know the word of God or even read the Bible? Have we taken up the gifts, fruits, and charisms of the Spirit to aid our fight? We have so many sacramentals to aid us, but do we take advantage of them?

As far as I can tell, the battle between God and Satan for our souls is only worsening. Our society is to the point where we sin and think we are right in doing so. This is what the devil feeds off of, especially when we offer the human sacrifice of abortion. When we take any action, we need to consider whom we are serving. Every sin marks us for the evil one. We need to stand fast for God; otherwise, the devil will claim us for his own. I, for my part, do not want to be dragged along to hell because of any apathy, any feeling of "I'll let others do the fighting for me" and then discover that they didn't fight hard enough. Can I save my family or myself? No, but God can. As long as I depend on him and make my allegiance to him, I don't need to worry. I'll ask our Mother Mary to stand with me and defend me, and I know she'll keep us all wrapped in her mantle. Hmm, the mantle of Mary. I think with our Lady's mantle as my armor I'll have everything I need.

"Finally, draw your strength from the Lord and from his mighty power. Put on the armor of God so that you may be able to stand firm against the tactics of the devil. For our struggle is not with flesh and blood but with the principalities, with the powers, with the world rulers of this present darkness, with the evil spirits in the heavens" (Eph. 6:10–12).

BOUNDARIES

"Why your mommy not letting us go past the yellow line?" I overheard my four-year-old daughter's friend ask her. She was asking about the yellow line we have painted across the end of our drive-way. My daughter replied matter-of-factly, "Because she wants us to be safe."

"Why?"

"Because," my precocious girl explained, "There are cars on the road."

"Oh."

End of conversation, as if that explanation satisfied everything in the world. If we could only place the trust that our children have in us in our Father in heaven then we would accept without further explanation of needing to follow God's commandments because he wants us to be safe. If we go beyond the boundaries our Father laid down for us, then we could get hurt. He's not giving us rules to be a mean, vindictive Father, but because he sees like most parents when his children could be in danger.

Speaking of "founding fathers," I recently read a passage from John Adams that he wrote in June 1776:

> Statesmen, my dear Sir, may plan and speculate for Liberty, but it is Religion and Morality alone which can establish the Principles upon which Freedom can securely stand.
>
> The only foundation of a free Constitution is pure Virtue, and if this cannot be inspired into our People in a greater Measure than they have it now, They may change their Rulers and forms of Government, but they will not obtain a lasting liberty. (Straub 2011)

Adams is saying then that we are only truly free within the boundaries of religion and morality. It is up to us personally to maintain standards of virtue. But some might argue that those rules are too constraining and not meant for modern times. This is, after all, the twenty-first century. We've had the sexual revolution and can find drugs on practically any corner. Yet neither can we mention God in public schools nor teach basic moral values because someone's bound to say we're discriminating when we don't include every way of life and choice as a basic moral value. We wonder why families are falling apart in search of satisfying the all-important *I*. We've become such a disconnected society with everyone rampantly exploring their own liberty at the expense of those around them that we've forgotten our roots. Our country was founded with the concept of religious freedom not being squelched by government, but this is what we're coming dangerously close to these days.

We are only free and grow to our best potential if we stay within the bounds laid out by our Creator. He's set pretty high standards for us and expects us to live up to them. We need to help society strive toward a good that's higher than itself. Or should we live down to our lowest expectations where we tolerate everything and where everyone is "free" to live as they choose regardless of the consequences? What kind of a society do we want our children to inherit? Think about it. We're setting the example.

"I have set before you life and death, the blessing and the curse. Choose life, then, that you and your descendants may live, by loving the Lord, your God, heeding his voice, and holding fast to him" (Deut. 30:19–20).

Hold fast

> "Be on your guard not to be led into the error of the
> unprincipled and to fall from your own stability"
>
> (2 Pet. 3:17).

Traveling for a vacation always throws my system into shock. I admit I like my way of life. I like my schedules and activities. I love my group of friends. I cherish my prayer time. I also realize that *my* Christian sense of normalcy doesn't mesh with the rest of the world. That doesn't make me holier than thou, and it doesn't mean the world is teeming with evil people. I think many have just lost their way. I wonder if there is anyone who will show them the way back.

On my vacation, I can't say I met a single truly evil person. I did, however, meet lots of people who don't have a place for God in their lives. They all knew about God and maybe even attended church periodically, but they didn't live for him. I'm not applying this to everyone. Most were honestly trying, and thank heavens for them! But in general, isn't apathy how our world got itself into its current state? By people not concerned about living for God anymore? So now we have every abominable act the New Testament writers told us of and more. This dark haze covers the world, and it's hard to see God's light. When we venture beyond our doorsteps, we are deluged with apathetic attitudes and derision for our belief in God. Now is when we must hold on to our faith more than ever! I was only gone for one week, but I slacked off in my prayer time. I knew I wouldn't be able to pray alone as much as at home. Obviously, I went to visit and spent much time with family and friends, but I could feel the ache of not having a quiet time with the Lord. Prayer is what we need to help us think straight when faced with all the arguments of a faithless world. Prayer restores our energy and strengthens and invigorates us to keep up the fight for Christ in our lives. If we don't pray, soon we will start to see the way the world sees, and we won't notice it. Remember the frog wouldn't jump into boiling water, but if he got in when the water was cold, then he didn't notice the heat being turned up? Just like the frog, we are killing ourselves in our society gone awry.

We need to pray to keep ourselves focused on God, who is our Way, our Truth, and our Life. While practically every country in the world is trying to proclaim that there is no moral truth and values are relative to people's opinions, we Christians need to stand firm and be God's light, to let them know the temperature's rising. How will people know to call out for help if they don't realize something's wrong? It's so easy to say but so hard to do. Witnessing by example, if not by words, takes guts, especially to our own family and friends. That's where we have to trust that God is bigger than we are and will speak for us. As long as we pray and stay close to him, he can use us to bring light to a darkening world.

How's our hearing

I often joke that there's an advantage to being the parent: we're bigger, stronger, and smarter than our kids, at least for the time being till they grow up! There are times when those things can be lifesavers. When we see our kids heading into danger, we can pull them back, literally sometimes, from collisions with oncoming cars, dogs, and other kids. It gets more difficult as they get bigger. We might call for them to stop, but sometimes they still need a tug on the arm to alert them. It was on one such occasion when I thought, what if I couldn't pull them back? What if I had to rely on just speaking and reasoning to get them to turn around? Would they listen?

Do we listen? Sometimes I wonder what possessed God to give us free will. He's given us the choice of which way to go, whether to follow him or to wander into danger. And when we do wander, he can only plead for us to come back. He can't necessarily grab us by the collar and yank us back because that would be interfering with our free will. I try to imagine myself standing in front of my daughters and trying to keep them out of danger just by pleading (and as they age it may come to that) and then watching them as they continue to drift further away. Now imagine our Father in front of us, begging and imploring us with a tear-stained face to turn around. Such agony for him to watch his precious children walking into darkness! How it lacerates his heart and deepens his wounds! His lips are parched and cracked from begging us, so now we must ask ourselves, do we listen? Do we help his thirst for souls, for our own soul in particular? This is why he's given us free will even though it causes him such suffering, so we may freely choose to love and follow him. A love that's coerced doesn't bring the sweet delight of a love freely chosen. After an argument with my daughters, I'm tickled to death to have them eventually turn around and give me this huge hug as if nothing happened. We can do the same thing. After wandering into the darkness, the sacrament of confession gives us the opportunity to give God a huge hug and mend the wounds of his heart. If we reach up to him a little, how he will hurry to reach down and pick us up, forgiving us instantly. Nothing delights him more than to shower us with mercy and grace and to rest our aching hearts in his, and his in ours, knowing that we've returned to him. There is nothing in the world that compares to the joy of loving God and being loved by him. Would that everyone knew that love! Let's consider where we are in relation to our Father now, and let's come back to him.

DID YOU HEAR?

"Child," said the Voice, 'I am telling you your story, not hers. I tell no-one any story but his own'" (Lewis 1970, 159).

"Curiosity killed the cat" or so the saying goes. Our curiosity and our inability to control ourselves causes us more problems than we dream. Some curiosity is good: If we weren't curious, how would explorers have ever sailed beyond the edge of the map or set foot on the moon? But we also need to learn how and when to curb that curiosity. Our desire to know every little tidbit of information about each other also leads to becoming town gossips. We already know the tongue is the hardest thing to control and brings many people to ruin (James 3). What is the hunger in us that wants to know about other people's lives? Do we feel like we have power over someone when we know about them?

Even Jesus told us not to be overly concerned with what goes in others' lives: "When Peter saw him, he said to Jesus, 'Lord, what about him?' Jesus said to him, 'What if I want him to remain until I come? What concern is it of yours? You follow me'" (John 21:21–22). We so much want to make it our business to know everything about each other. We put forth our unwarranted opinions (sometimes just to be part of a conversation), which usually contain judgments. Think about our conversations about politicians. We love to say, "If I were them…," and we all have our own perfect solutions. Yet despite a politician's, or our neighbor's, stand, we don't know each other's stories, the details that have shaped their lives, and why they make decisions they do. Who are we to make an opinion, criticism, or judgment against them? (How dare I write about such a subject when I have such troubles myself? I write not from the perspective of someone who's conquered the matter but from someone who's still struggling to learn.) St. Peter said that even the angels, who are greater than us, don't dare to pass judgment (2 Pet. 2:11) Let God, who knows people's stories, give to each the judgment they deserve: "'Vengeance is mine, I will repay,' says the Lord" (Rom. 12:19). If we regard each other as superior to ourselves (Phil. 2:3), even if we feel justified for being right, we will be changed. We can start giving people the benefit of the doubt and building them up. We'll begin to recognize when something should or shouldn't be said. Yes, our conversations may be quieter, but perhaps it will help us to do our job here on earth better, which is to love. May God our Father have mercy on us all!

UNITY IN PRAYER

The stillness of the Poor Clare monastery's chapel was broken only by the rustling of pages turning and rosary beads clinking as one by one the nuns filter in for morning prayer. As one nun fixed her gaze upon the altar, her heart swelled as she heard the barefoot *pat, pat* of another also coming to kneel, kiss the floor, and lift her heart to her Lord, loving the same God she herself has chosen to love. There is community here, and oneness as their voices spiral toward heaven, "Lord, open my lips…"

Across the world, men and women have formed communities of religious who dedicate their lives to loving God in various forms. It is they who are the heartbeat of the church with their constant prayer. The prayer binding them together, the Liturgy of the Hours, is also meant to be shared by everyone. According to *Novo millennio ineunte* by Pope St. John Paul II, a communal spirit must be shared between clergy, religious, and laity alike. "We need to promote a spirituality of communion," to think of our brothers and sisters within the faith as "those who are a part of me" (2001). How are we supposed to share the sorrow of people in war-torn areas half a world away when we're living comfortably in the US? Sometimes it's very easy to say yes, we are the body of Christ, but not feel connected in any way. It's through public prayer that we are reminded we "are in touch with all mankind and can contribute in no small degree to the salvation of the whole world" (Catholic Church, 27) Praying is one way to have an empathy with the people around us, especially if we're all joining in the same prayer. John Paul II called us to discover that we are part of a community, and as such, we have a responsibility to help each other grow toward Christ. All the baptized are called to holiness, whether in formal community life, families, or individually. The church highly recommends that the family, the domestic church, should pray the Divine Office together in the home as well.

There's a rhythm to the Divine Office that becomes familiar. How many of us though, if there's a vesper service in church, recognize the pattern of psalms, readings, and petitions as part of the office? Do we have a sense of familiarity with it and realize it's the same prayer Catholics across the world are chanting that evening? It's comfortable knowing that this is what the rest of the church is praying right now, rather like going to Mass in another state and still knowing all the responses. This form of prayer promotes the unity desired by Christ since we gather as one body and pray for the whole. In this way we grow closer not only to others within the church, but we bind ourselves closer to our God as every day we spend some time in prayer with him. This is one of the ways to "let the word of Christ dwell in you richly…singing psalms, hymns, and spiritual songs with gratitude in your hearts to God" (Col. 3:16).

THE DIGNITY OF WORK

"Time to get up and make the doughnuts," or so the saying goes, meaning it's time to get to work, whatever form it takes. It seems many people simply don't enjoy their work and see it as drudgery. If that's the case and there's no joy in work, there's going to be no joy in the rest of one's life. Sometimes it's simply too hard to get up and face the rest of the day. Don't feel you're alone if you're one of these people. People have been despairing over the workweek since biblical times! In the Liturgy of the Hours, the first psalm on Monday of week 1 is Psalm 5. It begins

> "To my words give ear, O Lord,
> give heed to my groaning.
> Attend to the sound of my cries."

Either the editors had a sense of humor or they weren't morning people either. Maybe reading through morning prayer can give us the boost we need to get going. God hears all prayers, even the psalms of complaint!

Perhaps why work is given such a bad rap is because we've not considered the true nature of work. If we go back to Genesis, we see that God made us in his image and put us on the earth to subdue it. Work was not a penalty; man was supposed to be imitating God in his work of creation, and God saw his work as good. So "from the beginning therefore he is *called to work. Work is one of the characteristics that distinguish* man from the rest of creatures" (John Paul II 1981, intro.). The basic definition of *work*, according to *Webster's Dictionary*, is "activity in which one exerts strength or faculties to do or perform something." Regardless of the job we have, the fact that we work means we are yet assisting in God's work of creation. Hopefully, we can look at our work and say, "It is good."

Our best example of work is the holy family itself. Joseph and Mary were workers, Joseph at his carpentry and Mary in the home. Jesus himself followed his step-father's work as a carpenter although the Bible doesn't mention whether he was good at it or not. Perhaps that's why he became a preacher! The fact is Jesus wanted his life to be an example for us to follow, and he chose to work. He knew the balance between work and rest because, like His Father in heaven who rested when his work was done, Jesus would go to an out of the way place to rest and pray.

Sometimes there's a tension between work and prayer when our work seems to be taking away from our prayer life. While it's a good and necessary thing to have a certain time during the day for only prayer, we need to allow our work to be prayer as well. In her Rule of Life, St. Clare of Assisi wrote, "Let the sisters to whom the Lord has given the grace of working work faithfully and devotedly…Let them do this in such a way that, while they banish idleness, the enemy of the soul, they do not extinguish the Spirit of holy prayer and devotion to which all other things of our earthly existence must contribute" (Mastrorilli 2003).

If we offer our work to God, be it delegating office tasks, milling tools, or watching kids and scrubbing the floor, then our work becomes prayer and our minds more in union with him. Our work is a reflection of who we are, so we need to enjoy our work to help us love more completely. There needn't be tension; we simply let our lives, work, and rest, become one joyful act of love and prayer offered to God. This isn't a practice that's done once and is over. It's something which takes a lifetime to do. Let's begin today with remembering God at an unlikely time during our work and taking a couple a seconds to say, "This is for you, my Lord." Then do it again and again and again.

SETTING AN EXAMPLE

> My anger protected me only for a short time; anger wearies itself out and truth comes in.
>
> —Martindale and Root

Last week, on my way home from work, I was so mad, I could've spit nails. I work with kids in the schools and two of the kids I work with had the same problem that day: they were hungry. These aren't teenagers or even later elementary who can fend for themselves. These are small children who depend on their parents. So needless to say, I was mad at the parents for a whole list of reasons. These kids, and countless more like them, need so much. Not only do they need food and the basic necessities of life, they need love, compassion, someone to trust, and someone to hold them when they're scared. So where are the parents? I thought. But then I looked at the adult figures in their lives, and then I realized I was looking at children in adult bodies.

Somewhere along the line, these adults had never received what they cannot give their children. So then I go back to their parents and further and further back, but when do we stop placing the blame that the kids just weren't raised right? Excuses won't change a situation; someone needs to stand up and be accountable.

As I was praying, trying to understand all this, I read Titus, chapter 2 in the Bible. It's so short but it speaks volumes. For example, verses 3–5 state, "Similarly, older women should be reverent in their behavior, not slanderers, not addicted to drink, teaching what is good, so that they may train younger women to love their husbands and children, to be self-controlled, chaste, good homemakers, under the control of their husbands, so that the word of God may not be discredited." That's just one example of the responsibility we have! So before I go looking too hard at other people, I need to make sure I'm doing my own job well. There are times when I feel overwhelmed because God is so beautiful, and we are so stained in our nature. How could we ever come close to him or be pleasing in his eyes? That's when I desperately grab hold of his mercy and trust, and pray that I'm trying my hardest as I know how with my own family, and I hope that's acceptable.

Now, Father, please help me to help someone else. I can't help them all, but I can at least hold them in my heart and offer them to you, and say please let them know they are loved. Then I'll go back to my two little clients and teach them what I know about you. One life at a time, Father. One little life at a time.

Pummeled hearts

"He piled upon the whale's white hump the sum of all the general rage and hate…as if his chest had been a mortar, he burst his hot heart's shell upon it"

(Lombardi 2014).

I've been reminding myself frequently these days of phrases like "all things change" and "this too shall pass." Anything to keep light at the end of the tunnel, hmm? I love mothering, but I never said it was easy. Oh no.

One of my daughters has been going through a stage of angry outbursts over the tiniest little things. While trying to get at the root of the matter, we endure episodes of ranting and screaming, kicking, hitting, etc. She'll be shoving me one minute, shouting, "Go away," and then an hour later be curling up on my lap just wanting to sit. Needless to say, by day's end, I feel a bit pummeled. So when I take it to God, what does he do? He shows me how he's in the exact same position. (The way God works is really quite amazing; the lessons are awesome.)

The Father tells us he loves us so much that he sent Jesus to be sacrificed, to bring us back home to heaven. But we are so much like our children when we go to confession and tell Jesus that we love him and then go out and turn away from him in sin. To God, our sin is like those hits and kicks. So we go back to confession and tell him we love him, and of course, he'll tell us that he forgives us and loves us, what parent wouldn't? Yet our sins are crucifying Jesus all over again, and he still says that he loves us. He still forgives. *Nothing* will ever change that. That's what our love looks like as a parent because we will always love our children no matter what they do.

I have to marvel at God's wisdom and his mercy. He is so much our Father, and so perfectly understands the ways of children. He knows that we get angry and sometimes do things just to spite him out of anger. Oh, we don't always know we do it, just like a child. All we know is we get mad at something or someone, and the abuse comes out. Our Father, knowing that our tantrums will pass, calmly holds us (just like a parent holds their child while they're a little ball of fury) and accepts the violence we fling on him. And then, when we're spent and have nothing left save exhausted tears, we fall into our Father's outstretched arms and he holds us, he just holds us. He loves us; we are his. He loves us, and he'll forgive us if we ask. We just have to desire it.

I praise God every day for his boundless mercy and the gift of forgiveness he offers. Let's never take it for granted. Remember, this is a time of mercy. His justice will most likely come next and when we least expect it. For now, let's learn all we can of our Father's virtues and imitate them in dealing with our family and friends. Maybe it will make the world not quite such an angry place.

THE CRY OF THE POOR

For one very specific moment of history God heard His people when they cried, "How long, Lord?...How long will you hide your face from me?" (Ps. 13:2). They were waiting for God to send them a messiah, someone to deliver them from the hands of their oppressors. God heard the deepest meaning of their cry, and he sent them his Son to deliver them from the bonds of slavery to sin. In Jesus, God showed them the way to have a better life among themselves, a way to live in peace and wisdom. How well did they respond to the message Jesus had for them? God answered their cry, but for some he didn't answer the way they wanted.

Again today we cry to God, "How long must we wait? When will you send us peace?" God still hears us, and he still gives the answer in the example Jesus gave. He tells us, with eyes firm yet gentle, "You cry to me, 'Have mercy on us,' but I say, 'You be merciful. You ask me to clothe the naked and feed the hungry. You clothe the naked. You feed the hungry. It does no good for me to miraculously give the poor food because the world won't be any better for it. If you want the world to change, your hearts have to change. I will not be outdone in generosity, but will you be generous as well? Will you give until you're poor? I allow some people to be rich and some poor to see how you would use your wealth. Will you share or will you think only of yourselves? If you sincerely desire me to help others, you will allow me to act in you. You pray for my kingdom to come. It can't come until you truly want it to. Unite your will to mine. Be perfected, just as I am perfect. Then the world will change according to your prayer because, together, we have willed it so. I gave you the best example of how to live my will in Jesus. Follow him. He is the Way, the Truth, and the Life.'"

God gave us the answer to our prayers personified in Jesus. How willing are we to accept that answer? The Lord hears the cry of the poor. Blessed be the Lord. Blessed are we when we hear the cry of the poor and act on it.

A WORD OF ENCOURAGEMENT

I've just returned from a mission trip in the northern Appalachian Mountains where my family and I spent a week in service. It was a fantastic experience, and I was delighted to hear my girls asking if they could go again. The work was hard, both physically and spiritually, but the rewards are outstanding. I'll just focus on one aspect of the week that you wouldn't think would make that much of a difference, but the results were amazing. One activity that we did every day was to write a little note of encouragement to others on our team, nothing big, just a couple of lines. I can't comment on the effect reading them had on people, but I can mention the effect writing them had on me.

Most of the time, you go to work with people you see and interact with so often, you don't consider their uniqueness anymore. In Appalachia, we were formed into groups where we didn't know many other people. We were supposed to write notes to everyone on our team, naming something positive, so I had to pay attention to my interactions with them and how they worked and interacted with others. This was challenging. How often do we really look for the positive in people, knowing that we'd actually have to tell them? So many times, it's easy to find the negative because it's something that annoys us or we just can't wait to tell some gossip. If they're doing something we like or we're working well together, we don't seem to notice and forget to make a positive comment. But if we have an assignment, suddenly we pay attention and try to find the good attributes. The next thing we know, we're looking at people differently and trying to find the good things God made in them and trying to overlook their faults. Wouldn't it be amazing if we did that every day? How would our interactions with people change?

At one point in the week, our assignment broadened, and we had to find the positive in the people we were going to work for and tell them sometime before we left for the day. Their reactions were amazing. We got everything from little grins and head nods to tears. Something in the human spirit reacts to hearing the truth. The biggest reactions came from the people it was hardest to find something nice to say about.

As I considered all this and the way it made me look at people, I wondered what would happen if more people had to find the good in others (as if they were going to tell them), and how it might change our homes, workplaces, and neighborhoods. It changes us for one, but if we start telling people the good that's in them, well, how might our world change?

THE TOUCH OF GOD

I stopped believing in coincidences a long time ago. There are just too many wonderful things that happen to be explained as chance. My most recent one was a couple of days ago, when my oldest daughter got a letter stating she could go en pointe in ballet this fall (a dream she's had for many years). When I asked my youngest daughter if there was anything she'd like to try, she reeled off a few ideas and immediately rejected them. Then she landed on painting lessons. Good grief. That's not exactly like signing up for dance or music after school. Where would I find art lessons? "Okay, Father, you've got to help me find them." That afternoon, a lady, who lived half a mile down the road, came to my door, looking for her lost cat. We started talking and then she says "I teach art lessons, painting specifically." I grinned. "Really?" Wow, talk about prayers answered quickly! My husband had overheard our conversation and just stood there shaking his head, saying he couldn't believe it. God is good.

Why is it so hard to believe that God answers such little prayers, or that he's close enough to have a hand in our daily lives? If we whisper prayers under our breath all the time, should we not expect an answer? Jesus did teach us to ask for our daily bread. He didn't just mean food. It also means the little things that we need throughout the day, spiritual or physical. Our God is right here. He's walking with us, touching us through our day. The more we get used to him knowing our every word and action, the more we expect him to be a part of our lives, and the more we can live in expectant faith. Of course, prayers won't always be answered yes. We have to take God on his terms, and there will be plenty of nos, but we'll come to see those as answers as well. What's even better is if we live knowing that he's with us (just picture him standing by your side in everything you do). Soon our thoughts, words, and actions will begin to change. "Do I really want to do/say that with my Father watching?" Soon it won't be an obligation to please him because, with God living so close to us, we can't help but grow in love with him, and we want him to be pleased. If we let him, he touches our lives as surely as Jesus touched the people around him to heal them and as surely as he physically touches us in the Eucharist (such in intimate embrace!). Jesus still touches us today. Allow ourselves to be delighted in the touch of our God and respond to him throughout the day. Mold ourselves to him; watch how our lives convert to his heart's desires. As we eat more and more of his daily bread then we'll understand more of "thy will be done." Blessed be God forever!

Day by Day

The pain now is part of the happiness then.

—*Shadowlands*, 1993

Summer was too short! That's the lament I've heard most often the past few weeks, and my own voice added to it. We've waited so long for drier, warmer weather, and when it finally came, the changing leaves arrived with it. But then that's life, isn't it? We spend so much time waiting for something else to happen. And then, when the something else does happen, it isn't what we wanted it to be and wish we could go back. It seems at times that life passes us by so quickly, we can hardly catch our breath. Jesus had it right when he told us, "Do not worry about tomorrow; tomorrow will take care of itself. Sufficient for a day is its own evil" (Matt. 6:34). We have such a hard time being happy where and when we are, yet this is what God has given us. A story which comes to mind is that of St. Francis. While he was working in his garden, St. Francis was asked what, if he knew the world would end in an hour, would he choose to be doing? St. Francis replied that he would still be working in his garden because it was where God had placed him in that moment.

I find myself amazed at the life and responsibility God has given me. I have two giggly little girls who are growing like weeds. They are small only a few precious years, and I know when they wrap their arms around my neck in Velcro hugs it won't last. I thank God for their hugs and delight in every one of them. I wouldn't trade them for anything. I pray that God will use the good times to strengthen me and sustain me during times of sorrow. I cling to the Christian hope of eternity with God. In doing so, I discover an ability to take life with its daily hardships and joys and offer it all to him. In as much as I am able, I offer up a life fully experienced, soaked up, and none wasted. I try not to be too anxious about what could happen. I place it all in Jesus's hands (Jesus, I trust in you!). And I pray that I live in the present I'm given, not bemoaning the "if onlys" and "could have beens." Sometimes this too can take a monumental effort with God-given strength to do. But in the end, there is peace, and in peace, joy.

I can't change a too wet and cool summer, but I can enjoy the upcoming fall with its colors and smells. Winter may be coming, but its approach makes fall all the more treasured.

BEING HIS GARDEN

> Without prayer I could not work for even half an hour. I get my strength from God through prayer.
>
> —Mother Teresa

One of my favorite things to do in summer is work in my garden. I love the feel of the soil and smell of the plants. I like weeding and clearing space for my plants to grow (although my girls give me dubious looks when I have them help weed). Reaping the benefits of hard work is satisfying and cheaper on the grocery bill. But for me, the best part of gardening is the silence and prayer. The lessons God gives, I'm starting to share with my girls while we work, and it's fun to see their faces set in thought as they rationalize the lessons. God uses simple tools to teach us, like gardening, but sometimes we lose the lessons in life's complexities. For example, let's take prayer.

Once the soil is tilled, watered, planted and starting to produce, we have to weed. How do we know what to weed? What's the difference between a potato and a weed? The more we garden, the more we come to know the difference between weeds and garden plants. The more we pray, the better we know in our own lives which habits or influences are weeds, and which are good fruit-bearing graces. But like gardening, if we don't pray, we won't know. Through prayer we recognize those vices which need to be eliminated. The soil absorbs the sun and rain and gives plants nourishment. Prayer is our strength and nourishment. It helps us to recognize and absorb God's graces and blessings and use them well. Prayer is the foundation that gets us through the day, helps us to meet any challenge, and respond appropriately. When my girls have one of their spats or are just being stubborn, I can respond fairly calmly and figure out the root of the problem rather than simply reacting (negatively) to their outbursts. Which, without prayer, I couldn't do. Prayer lets us recognize whether we should listen or lecture when problems arise and allows us to act with a heart bent on God's will, not on our own.

In the garden, I hoe and prune in order to help plants grow. The weeds and branches thrown to the side remind me that God's pruning me all in the name of love. I want my garden to grow. He wants me to grow closer to him. Pruning can be painful even when the purpose is understood. That's when I look to the bigger picture: eternal life with God. I stand in my garden and look at all the vegetables that I'll preserve and will last me through the year. Then I look to Jesus, and I know he's working in me to get me ready for eternal life with him. Prayer is the very air I breathe: the longing for Jesus, the turning of our eyes to heaven and the catch in our breath, the waiting to be united with the God who loves us, that desire is prayer. If we don't pray, how can we recognize God anywhere in our lives? Yes, prayer takes time, and sometimes it's hard to pray. Then so is gardening. But the rewards are so worth it. The fruit of gardening feeds my body. The fruit of prayer feeds my soul. Without both, we would die, plain and simple. Let us praise the Lord for creating us to pray!

THE ASSUMPTION OF THE BLESSED VIRGIN MARY

We don't know how long the Virgin Mary lived after Jesus ascended into heaven; different sources say she lived to her early sixties. Scriptures mention her in the upper room at Pentecost, and some scholars say that she spent her last days with St. John in Ephesus, Turkey, but that is the last mention of the Mother of God. The *Catechism of the Catholic Church* states, "Finally the Immaculate Virgin...when the course of her earthly life was finished, was taken up body and soul into heavenly glory, and exalted by The Lord as Queen over all things" (966). When Jesus gave his mother to John at the foot of the cross, she became the mother of us all through her unique sharing in the passion of her son. As mother, Mary continually helps us to come closer to God and gains grace for us. None of the grace originates from her; it's all from God. But because she so perfectly lived and cooperated with God's plan for her, Mary is full of grace as the angel Gabriel greeted her in Luke 1:28. When Mary was assumed into heaven, her job wasn't completed. The Mother of God continues her role as intercessor into the modern day with her various apparitions throughout the centuries.

Overall, apparitions are private revelation; no one has to believe in them. Several have been found worthy of belief by the church (for example, Lourdes and Fatima), and we may participate in what they advocate or not without penalty of sin. It's a personal choice. Approved apparitions, and there are many over the centuries, are beautiful examples of God's mother as a messenger to us, his children.

Nothing Mary says ever contradicts the gospel. In every apparition, her instructions and encouragement are simply intended to bring us closer to him through various means. Not once has the Virgin ever suggested breaking away from or starting another church. In every way, Mary points toward God by means of faithfulness to the church, its priests, and the pope.

"The serpent, however, spewed a torrent of water out of his mouth after the woman to sweep her away with the current" (Rev. 12:15). Anyone who defends God these days practically takes their life in their hands. Snickers might be the least they endure. If God called someone in the role of prophet, often times the person is outright rejected. Various visionaries and locutionists are accused of being brainwashed; however, there can't be apparitions without visionaries, and visionaries are human. While people themselves may have faults, God has none. Any true message seems to get through unharmed even though it may take a while for the approval. This does not mean the visionaries are suddenly divine and worthy of belief. The apparition is. This problem goes back to Paul in his first letter to the Corinthians. He says quite plainly, "Was Paul crucified for you? Or were you baptized in the name of Paul?" (1 Cor. 1:13). As soon as people start following the visionary and not to whom the visionary is pointing, there are divisions. It's entirely contrary to what God intends.

Sometimes another contention point is the behavior of visionaries during apparitions, such as ecstasies or other charisms. We are mortal, God is divine. Sometimes there's a reaction between the two. This also has been occurring since Old Testament times. It was recognized that someone in special communication with God was changed. "The spirit of the Lord will rush upon you, and you will join them in their prophetic state and will be changed into another man" (1 Sam. 10:6). It is not, however, a sign of an apparition's authenticity. We should simply be aware that the intensity of prayer can change one's behavior physically and mentally.

With these thoughts in mind, let us ask God to help us in our discernment of alleged apparitions and follow the guidance of the church. Jesus created a beautiful bride, and she's withstood two thousand years of testing. Attacks on our Lady's apparitions and the hierarchy were all foreseen by him and won't last. Holy Mary, Mother of God and our mother, pray for us!

HINDSIGHT

How often do we think if we only knew then what we know now, things would've been different? What about Mary? Would Mary have said yes?

We know Mary now as the Queen of Heaven, but what did she know during Jesus's life and her life on earth? Suppose she had no divine revelation apart from Gabriel's Ave? Perhaps we could assume that Mary knew of the prophecies predicting a victorious messiah king and also a suffering servant. The Jews thought they referred to two different people. Was Mary expecting the victorious king when Gabriel announced that her baby would have the throne of David? Scriptures didn't say he would be born in power or wealth, and David himself came from humble origins as a shepherd. Why couldn't this king have a humble beginning as well? Mary and Joseph wouldn't have been surprised at the events surrounding his birth then, after all, he was the future Messiah. As for the quiet years in Nazareth, Mary and Joseph probably treasured all of life's tender moments and lessons in their hearts. Did Jesus give any kind of inkling as to what kind of king he would be? Were they waiting for an anointing like David's? Perhaps Mary thought she was seeing prophecy fulfilled when Jesus began his public life and had a large following. As she hung on his every word, did his predictions of his own death and resurrection frighten or mystify her? How prepared was she for his passion? As her maternal heart was breaking, did another part of her realize that her son Jesus was still God and could choose to walk away any time he wished? And yet he didn't. Instead of coming as someone powerful, which we cannot all hope to be, he came as one weak and poor, which we all can be. Did the realization that the victorious king and suffering servant were one person come crashing down on Mary? When her anguished heart accepted that her God underwent this torture and death willingly for all our sake, did it drive her to her knees to utter again yes at the foot of his cross? Whether or not Mary understood all the events at the time doesn't lessen the fact that she still gave God her all.

Do we understand God's plans for us? Do we immediately see the big picture? Most likely not, but with God's grace, we can say yes to whatever we face in our lives, just like Mary did all those years ago. Sweet heart of Mary, be our salvation!

ANGELS BEFORE US

As the seasons turn to autumn, Ordinary Time continues, but more feasts and remembrances start to fill the days. September 29 is the feat of the Archangel Michael, Gabriel, and Raphael, and October 2, the Feast of the Guardian Angels.

Books on angels, angel statues, television programs with angels—angels do seem to be surrounding us, don't they? Many times, angels are portrayed in the role of messenger, giving the "Fear not, God loves you" tidings. In Psalm 103:20, we see the angels are those who "Bless the Lord…mighty in strength and attentive, obedient to every command." God created three hierarchies, each with three choirs, each choir having specific duties. In the hierarchy of all created things, we humans are below the angels but above animals, each level up getting closer to the perfection of God. So how do we, who are lower than angels, dare to call them our servants as well?

God, in his awesome divinity, knows all things, and when he made his creation, he knew about sin and knew he would send his Son as a human. By Jesus's becoming human, for a while being lower than the angels, he has elevated us to being God's adopted children, the heirs of salvation (Heb. 1, 2). (Lucifer, the beautiful "morning star, son of the dawn," [Isa: 14:12] was so prideful that he couldn't bear the thought of serving someone less. He lost that battle of the wills, essentially saying "I will not serve.") Since humans are the heirs of such a treasure, God sent angels to be our servants as well.

Some examples of how angels serve are seen in the Bible. The Archangel Gabriel came to Zechariah and Mary to deliver the message about the births of John the Baptist and Jesus. Raphael was sent to heal Tobit and Sarah in the Old Testament. Daniel, when he was found unharmed in the lion's den, stated, "My God has sent his angel and closed the lion's mouths so that they have not hurt me" (Dan. 6:23). Here we see angels in perhaps their most popular role, the defense of humans against evil. We call on St. Michael to defend us in battle against the wickedness and snares of the devil. The Prayer to St. Michael the Archangel, composed by Pope Leo XIII in 1884, was to be said after every mass. This practice was abolished in 1964, but considering the state of affairs in the world today, perhaps this prayer might be worth reinstating.

According to the Bible, God has also given us guardian angels to watch over each person individually. There are quite a few saints, such as Padre Pio, who were given the gift of being able to commune with their angel. It was even said that St. Pio would send his angel on errands. Most of us don't have that ability, but we can pray to our angels and ask their help and protection. They are there to help guide us to heaven. How do we know that Lucifer hasn't also dispatched his demons to each of us to try and help us on the opposite way? If, with the eyes of the spirit, we could see the battleground of spirits on which we stood, we might pray all the more passionately to God and his angels to be our strength on the journey. Let's not overlook the gift we've been given in the angels. If we join forces, perhaps evil can be overcome that much more quickly.

"St. Michael, the Archangel, defend us in battle. Be our protection against the wickedness and snares of the devil. May God rebuke him, we humbly pray, and do thou, O Prince of the heavenly host, by the power of God, cast into hell Satan and all the evil spirits, who prowl about the world seeking the ruin of souls."

OUR GUARDIAN ANGELS

I was recently at a Eucharistic celebration which, while beautifully done, was very poorly attended. However, what was lacking in numbers was made up for in enthusiasm: the response to prayers and singing was louder than at a Sunday Mass. As I was contemplating this situation, it occurred to me that the church was far from empty. We were joined by myriads of angels exulting in adoration before the Eucharist. Oh, the beauty of those angels as I imagined them! They could see plainly what we must take on faith, that Jesus is truly present in the Host before us. Since time doesn't exist for angels, the sacrifice on Calvary is present to them, and they know the gift we were given.

In addition to the Eucharist, God has given us a gift in the angels. They are such a wonderful resource for us, and we use them so little! The mission of the choir of angels right now is to assist us in coming to know the love of God and to see him face to face. They know the truth and want us to know it as well. But how do we tap this resource? The same way we accomplish anything: through prayer. We hear God's voice speaking to us in silence, and it's the same with angels. They will make their presence felt and give us little nudges in our conscience to let us know which way to go. Is it hard to think of angels, these exquisitely beautiful spirits before the throne of God, as servants to us? Yet that's what God's plan is. God lifted us up (who were lower than the angels) by his becoming part of physical creation through the birth of Jesus, who was robed in the flesh of Mary. This was the test of the angels and what divided them: the position of humans would be exalted over the angels by having God join himself to us and not the angels. It was too much for some, and so they fell from the heavens (Rev. 12). Now the angels who were obedient to God's plan are committed to helping us pass our own test: to be obedient to God's will. All we have to do is make room for their influence in our lives. Angels are aware of the free will that God gave us and, in their humility, would never infringe upon us unless we ask. However, the fallen angels, or demons, have no such inhibitions. They will attack us in whatever way possible. Don't hesitate to employ your guardian angel. Why else would God have assigned them to us? But always be humble, just as your angel is, because we have a gift they can never be granted—the Eucharist. They have no physical bodies, and God did not become an angel, yet they know how he took on human form and love him more than we can comprehend. What the angels must experience when they watch us receive communion with indifference! Ask them to help us to know Jesus in the Eucharist so that we too can come to know the truth with them. Then when we human spirits leave our earthly bodies, we can join our angelic companions in heaven, singing glory and praise to God.

Evil at work

Sometimes, people irritate us. Oh, they don't mean to be irritating, they just are. And I'm sure we're just as irritating right back. Sometimes we even do it on purpose. St. Paul sure had it pegged right when he said to bear with one another (Col. 3:13). This is a man who speaks from personal experience. He knows the damage that can happen when little cracks in relationships become larger rifts. Just read his letters. The devil knows what happens too, and he grabs on hold to any little annoyance he can to make it big. Sowing discord is what he does, and he does it well as we see in our world today. How easily we fall into the snares of the devil and become his tools. He rejoices over every soul torn from our Father's heart and brought to damnation. Have we considered how much we help his goal when we allow ourselves to hold onto even the smallest of grudges? Evil will find a crack and dig in its claws, not letting go until planted in our hearts are feelings of animosity, resentment, ideas of retaliation, and blotting out reasons to forgive. We get so caught up in the day-to-day business of life that sometimes we don't realize what's happening. We don't realize that those ill feelings are part of a war between God and the devil for our souls. We think it's just us, part of our human nature, and some of it probably is. But part of it also is the spiritual battle, and this part needs all the help we can give it. Just because passionate Christians seem to be in the minority these days doesn't mean we can play dead because it's easier. Not only do we need to pray for ourselves and our world, we need to employ the prayers of the saints in heaven who've won their battle and our guardian angels. Our guardian angels can see the spiritual aspect of the battles that we can't and can therefore put up a better defense. God gave them to us to guard us, but how much better if we asked them ourselves? We work better with people we know, and in the same way, we need to build a relationship with our angels.

Another option we have is recruiting St. Michael, the archangel. The prayer to St. Michael was suppressed along with other prayers to simplify the Mass, but could the exclusion of such a powerful prayer have been a small victory for the devil? Overall, it seems to be a sign that we've forgotten there is a battle being waged. This is a favorite tactic of the devil—we won't fight something that doesn't exist. It makes it easier for him to win. It wouldn't hurt us to start saying the St. Michael prayer again on our own. We need to use every tactic we can: the Eucharist, prayer, sacramentals, everything we can to show that we are God's children, and we won't go down without a fight. Glory to God forever!

"Although this prayer (St. Michael the Archangel) is no longer recited at the end of Mass, I ask everyone not to forget it and to recite it to obtain help in the battle against the forces of darkness and against the spirit of this world" (John Paul II 1994, sec. 4).

OUR TRUE COLORS

As I write, I'm sitting outside surrounded by rust-colored leaves that are past their peak, about half of which are fallen and stark branches showing through. I love the lessons nature teaches us, and when we distance ourselves from nature, we distance ourselves from a type of school. There are lessons to be learned here and wisdom gained. For example, did you know a leaf's true color isn't green? It's really the color we see in fall, when the light starts to fade and the chlorophyll lessens in the leaf. When we think the leaf is dying, it's actually just showing how it truly looks. So here's what I learned from this: when God showers us with so many graces—i.e., life is good—we look like that green leaf. We're all well-behaved and pleasant to be around, perhaps overflowing with compliments for others and being extra gracious. That's God loving us. But perhaps when we're not feeling

God's blessings and he seems farther away, we start to wither a little. The green, the niceties, fades from our souls, and our true selves start to assert themselves. When life isn't going our way, are we still as kind and cheerful to others or are we a tad sharper, more impatient, or more irritable? Maybe this is where God tests our true colors to see how well we still appear green to others even though we grit our teeth as we do so. This is us loving God. And then as I continue to look through the leaves and see the bare branches, this too, is our souls. When the leaves have all fallen, all that's left is a skeleton. When we've completely surrendered to our Father and he's annihilated us in him—when all the ornamentation has been stripped away, all the piety has been stripped away, and all that's left are our souls—what then remains but the faith, hope, and love that we've shown throughout our lives? The truest measure of ourselves will be how we treated others. How much did we love? And we cannot love if we do not have faith and hope in God. There is our skeleton, the bare bones of our souls. This is what our Father will look at when we stand before him, not how many devotions we did or how loudly we praised him. Those things are nice, but not essential.

Let's not be afraid to learn some lessons from nature. When we see what happens every fall to the trees—and they are only trees—perhaps when similar things happen to our souls, we won't be confused and wonder what's happening. We'll know and can apply examples we've seen elsewhere, and we'll know that maybe this is God working in our souls for our good. Then we can love him all the more for it. Blessed and praised be God forever!

PONDERING JESUS WITH MARY

I love the month of October. Not only is autumn in full swing, it's the month of the Rosary of our Lady. I realize that for many, the Rosary seems like mundane, repeated prayers that they just can't get into, but for some reason, I've been attracted to the Rosary since grade school. Maybe it's because I went to a Catholic school, and I thought all the sisters running around were like little Marys, and I loved their habits. Maybe it's because I learned about Fatima in fifth grade and that Lucia was still alive, and she had actually seen and spoken with the Virgin Mary, who lived two thousand years ago. The Lady asked us to pray the rosary, so I found a pamphlet and started saying it every day. If our mother should come from heaven and ask us to do something, I figured we'd better listen. She has so much to teach us.

The Son of God, who became the son of the Virgin, learned to pray in his human heart. He learns to pray from his mother, who kept all the great things the Almighty had done and treasured them in her heart (Catholic Church, 2599).

Mary prayed the way any Jewish woman of the time would pray. A lot of Jewish feast days have to do with remembering and pondering the works of God in their history. So as Mary pondered the works and mysteries of God in her own life, we are to follow her example. Jesus even told us we should "do this in remembrance" of him at the Last Supper when he gave us his body and blood. That's what every mass today is about, celebrating/remembering the covenant that Jesus ratified with his sacrifice, and also calling the Holy Spirit, the promise of the Father, to prepare us to receive him. The Holy Spirit also helps us to look forward to the kingdom of heaven, to stand before God face to face. The memory we have of Jesus's life on earth and the hope we have in Jesus's coming again, the hope of sharing life forever with him give us strength to live. Hope gives us the courage to endure whatever trial it is we're currently facing.

The Rosary, when prayed well and the mysteries pondered, is the perfect Marian prayer. When we share Jesus's life as seen by his mother, we share in their joys and sorrows, and we come to realize that Jesus and Mary are sharing in our life as well. That gives me hope to know that Jesus is feeling what I am feeling and helping me to get through it. This isn't a huge mystery of God only for theologians; this is what comes from quiet prayer and listening to our Lady. The only thing we have to do is just start, and wouldn't the month of the Rosary be a perfect time to do that? Jesus and Mary are waiting. Praised be, Jesus!

The scourge of the devil

Once when crossing an international border, a guard asked Mother Teresa if she was carrying any weapons. She pulled out her rosary and said, "Only this one" (Keucher 2010). What a wonderful response! Oh, to have wit like hers. While some might smile and leave Mother Teresa's response at that, we need to take pause and think. She's right and very serious about it. When we think of weapons, those that come to mind are the ones that do violence, yet the Virgin Mary has given us a most powerful and far more beautiful weapon: the rosary. Yes, the rosary truly does fit into the weapon category. Weapons have two purposes: first, to destroy the enemy, to be offensive in battle. We are in a deadly spiritual battle with the devil for our souls. Every time we contemplate with Mary in the Rosary, the face of Jesus the devil is infuriated. Pope Adrian VI said, "The rosary is the scourge of the devil" (Heilman, 2011). Lucia of Fatima explained that "the rosary and scapular are inseparable" (VanBuskirk 2010, 160). Francis of Yepes, brother of St. John of the Cross, had demons reveal to him that another weapon that torments them the most was the scapular of Our Lady of Mount Carmel: "'Take off that habit,' they cried to him, 'which snatches so many souls from us. All those clothed in it die piously and escape us'" (Catholics against Contraception 2001.) No soldier, and we are soldiers, would go into battle without the proper arms. How else would a soldier fight against falling into an enemy's hands? The second purpose of a weapon is self-defense. Self-defense involves learning skills for survival. As Catholic Christians we are up against pretty big odds. The world seems filled with hedonism, immorality, disregard for life, violence, drugs and despair. A strong family is our stability in this ocean.

"The Holy Rosary...has shown itself particularly effective as a prayer that brings family together. Individual family members, in turning their eyes to Jesus, also regain the ability to look one another in the eye, to communicate, to show solidarity, to forgive one another and to see their covenant of love renewed in the Spirit of God...they place their needs and their plans in His hands, they draw from Him the hope and the strength to go on" (John Paul II 2002, sec. 41).

Knowing all this, some may still think of the Rosary as a boring repetition of the Hail Mary, and indeed, if that's how one goes at it, that's all it will be—an empty shell. But think of it in human terms as our late holy Father invites us to do. I never get tired of hearing my daughters say I love you, no matter how often they tell me. Jesus assumed a human heart so he could speak to us in terms we humans understand. Three times Peter is asked, "Do you love me?" And the positive answer given three times, repeatedly. Like children wrapped in their Father's arms, we utter our human expressions of love over and over in the most perfect way possible, with Mary. For "although the repeated *Hail Mary* is addressed directly to Mary, it is to Jesus that the act of love is ultimately directed, with her and through her" (John Paul II 2002, sec. 26). Let's not be caught unarmed. If we take up our rosaries, we can destroy the enemy by heaping praises and words of love on Jesus through Mary. "Blessed is the fruit of thy womb, Jesus."

By any other name

It's said that a rose by any other name is still a rose. Halloween. Sounds like "All Hallow's Eve," doesn't it? In this case, the name remains the same, but I believe the holiday has changed. Do people dress up now to ward away evil spirits or do they emulate them? Do we receive soul cakes (doughnuts) in return for our prayers for the dead, or do children beg for candy simply for the sake of the candy? When I was growing up, Halloween, for me, was just a time to have fun dressing up and carving pumpkins. However, as I discovered what was supposed to be celebrated and what was actually being celebrated, the more disturbing it became. All Hallows' Eve (All Saints' Day) and All Souls' Day are the church's memorial day. During this time, we honor our loved ones who are already in heaven and praying for us, and those who are yet in purgatory, and we pray for them. Each country has their own traditions that sprang up in relation to the holiday, ranging from going to cemeteries to pray for the dead to the poor begging for food in return for prayers. In Mexico, picnics are held in graveyards, satirizing death, the enemy conquered by Christ. Yet somewhere along the way, a gradual transformation occurred. The focus point, honoring those souls who've escaped eternal death because of Christ, was shrouded in a glorification of that eternal death. Now the Christian element of salvation has been overshadowed by darkness.

Making the largest rise in culture today is the New Age movement (NAM), which is largely American based. For the sake of space and simplicity, the NAM is the rebirth of pagan religions. For them, Jesus was an enlightened leader of his time but no more. The earth is a living entity, etc. Those of a Wiccan philosophy as well as others have chosen Halloween as their high holy day. Now, where Christ is no longer highlighted, we have all sorts of pagan influences: witches and wizards, crystals, divination and horoscopes, superstition, charms, and more. Wherever we open the door a crack, the devil will sneak in, in innocent disguise, till we no longer know what it is we celebrate.

We can't fix what went wrong with Halloween in a year or two. What we can do is start praying to discern the good from the bad. Have the Halloween party but reconsider the focus. In all things, praise God because the devil can't stand it when we praise him. Through prayer we can "stand firm against the tactics of the devil. For our struggle is not with flesh and blood but with the principalities, with the powers, with the world rulers of this present darkness" (Eph. 6:11–12). Let's just be sure we know whom it is we're honoring before we celebrate any occasion.

SATISFYING OUR HUNGER

"Yes, the days are coming, says the Lord God, when I will send a famine upon the land: Not a famine of bread, or thirst for water, but for hearing the word of the Lord"

(Amos 8:11).

And a cry came up from the depths of their hearts, "How long, Lord?" (Ps. 13:2). How long must we wait? It is an anguished cry, wondering when the Lord would return, when the Lord would fix all that was wrong with the world and make a place that was beautiful and pure, when he would restore the lost Eden where we could once again walk with our God. We anxiously yearn for such a place, and we beg God to fix the world just like that, but are we ready for such a place? How many of us can honestly say in our own lives that we are ready to walk in such purity? How many of us have made any concrete attempt to prepare ourselves to live in his glory?

Our society is so filled with the cloud of wickedness that we've no idea how far it's crept into our homes and souls. We think nothing of what the media feeds us. Think of what's aimed at our teenagers and younger ones: vampires, bloodlust, spells, and sorcery are all the rage now in books and movies. We call it a fad, but what's this fad doing to our souls? Philippians 4:8 says, "Whatever is true, whatever is honorable, whatever is just, whatever is pure, whatever is lovely, whatever is gracious, if there is any excellence and if there is anything worthy of praise, think about these things." But why think about this stuff, we ask? It's boring. Instead we must think of it as health food for the soul. Because of our fallen nature, what's right may not taste as good as the junk, but it will keep us alive. This is the direct effect of sin—to rebel against whatever is good. But do we even realize or care that we are rebelling? In today's society, God is simply a concept to be embraced or left alone with no consequences for anyone. However, regardless of how society thinks of him, God is still God, he exists and so do we in relationship to him. God didn't create us to desire dark or perverse humor and violence. That's the work of the devil on us. Try to distinguish between the two pulls in our lives, what we watch or read, what we laugh at, and what we spend our time doing. Which do we hunger for more, light or darkness? When we've identified our hunger then, just like a diet, we learn to control our hunger. Pray, and with the Holy Spirit's help, we can give it new aim. The more we try to purify our lives, the more God will help us. Pray to our Blessed Mother because she is purity itself. She will hold us in the garden of her Immaculate Heart, pruning us and making us beautiful for God. Then we won't shrink from his radiance; we will be hungering for it.

PEP RALLIES

As the liturgical year dwindles, the beginning of November honors all the saints. The saints are those people we know to be in heaven because of miracles attributed to their intercession. I like to think of the saints as our cheerleaders, the cloud of witnesses who've achieved face-to-face union with God and are now encouraging us along our way. Reading their stories is our inspiration: their falls and risings, their human struggle to love the same God we love in a world of distraction. In our lives, as we undergo joy or sorrow, different saints will stand out for us and be our example. We'll look at them with excitement as we find similarities in our stories and can say, "Yes, I've experienced this as well."

GOD'S FOOL

"When the priest is offering sacrifice at the altar or the Blessed Sacrament is being carried around, everyone should kneel down and give praise, glory, and honor to our Lord God, living and true" (McCarthy 2010, 176). Written by St. Francis of Assisi to the superiors of his friars minor, these words reflect the evident love he had for Jesus and his enthusiasm in demonstrating that love. What a wonderful example of prayer we have in this little man from Assisi! St. Francis, whose feast we celebrate on October 4, gives us the witness we need to live for Christ unfettered by the world's opinions.

St. Francis started out life as a typical young Italian nobleman, basically partying without a care in the world. However, after hearing the call of Lady Poverty, he became a young man head over heels in love with Jesus Christ. He shed all of his father's wealth in a dramatic display, even shedding his clothes before his father's house.

From then on, he obeyed only Christ. He aided the poor, accepted no money, and had no possessions, served lepers, spent whole nights in prayer, and preached Christ. He was called a fool, yet he continued with his feet on the ground and eyes toward heaven. It was Francis' bonfire of faith that spread throughout the world as friary after friary popped up among nations. In addition to the Friars Minor, monasteries of Poor Ladies (later known as Poor Clares for their foundress) also began to spring up. Shortly after Francis's conversion, he asked Clare whether or not his main ministry should be to pray or to preach. After much prayer, Clare answered, "Preach" (Demaray 1992, 59).

If Francis preached with so much enthusiasm as to cause thousands of friars to join him, think of how much more intense his prayer life was. He would spend entire nights repeating a single mantra in his humility, "My God and my all!" Francis and his brother friars would lose themselves in the Spirit when they would speak so lovingly of God that once Jesus even appeared in their midst. Another time when he and St. Clare were eating together in the woods, the townspeople saw the woods on fire. When they arrived to put out the flames, they found Francis, Clare and their group lost in meditation on God. (Demaray 1992, 54–56). Imagine being so intent in your prayer that God would allow people to see flames!

Such a prayer life would be great to have but is, admittedly, a gift from God. Extraordinary things don't have to happen when we pray. Sometimes the most beneficial prayer is in the quiet stillness of our heart when we're lost in God and not disturbed by outside happenings. Sometimes we're so busy noticing what other people are doing that we forget to concentrate on God, and before we know it, our prayer time has slipped away. Perhaps we're too afraid others will notice us and how we pray, so we're afraid to stand, kneel, sing out, or lift our hands. In that case, maybe the first thing we need to ask God for is the true desire to pray and not care what others think. Most people aren't afraid to be seen clapping and cheering at a concert for another person; why should we be afraid that people will see us cheering in praise of God? Remember that St. Francis was called God's fool. If it's foolish to lift our hands and voices in praise and thanksgiving to our Father and creator, then may we all aspire to be God's fools!

BEING OURSELVES

It didn't take me long to figure out that my children's behavior is revenge for how I behaved as a child. My mom is in her glory when I tell of their latest antics only to have her tell similar tales of me. How we moms do like to compare stories, sometimes to others' dismay. "My child did this today." "Oh, well mine did that two months ago. Now he's doing this…" It's not like we're trying to one-up one another, but then sometimes we do it intentionally. Come to think of it, it's not just moms who do this either. "Love your glasses. I wish mine were like them," "If only I had a job like his…" We love to compare ourselves to everything and everybody. We can't seem to be happy with ourselves as we are. But why? My daughter asked, "Who do you love more, her or me?" Is this what it comes down to? That we want so much for people to love us or accept us that we feel we, as ourselves, aren't good enough? The best way to kill our souls is to compare ourselves to each other.

Unlike our workplaces where we are replaceable, God has given us all a specific task to accomplish during our lifetime. We cannot be somebody else and react with their reactions even if they are a saint. Imitating the saints can be daunting, not that they aren't great examples for us. God gave them the graces to do what they had to do. We can aspire to their goodness, as all good things come from God, but then we must take that desire for holiness and apply it to our own circumstances. There is a quote from St. Francis of Assisi that I love. At the end of his life, he told his brothers, "I have done what was mine to do. May Christ teach you what is yours." And as Blessed Mother Teresa said, we aren't called to do great things, but little things with great love.

St. Paul tells us, "Since we have gifts that differ according to the grace given to us, let us exercise them: if prophecy, in proportion to the faith; if ministry, in ministering; if one is a teacher, in teaching;

if one exhorts, in exhortation; if one contributes, in generosity; if one is over others, with diligence; if one does acts of mercy, with cheerfulness" (Rom. 12:6–8).

Sometimes we are so busy doing things throughout the day, we forget to ask God what it is we ought to be doing. Take time to read the scriptures. Go and spent a moment in Eucharistic adoration. Spending time before the Son is the best way to clear your mind and think. It really is necessary to spend time with God and not just doing things for him. It's where that peace in our soul will come from. As long as we are comparing ourselves to each other, we won't have that peace because someone will always be doing stuff better than we do. God doesn't need us to be someone else. He wants us to be us because no one can love him with our combination of qualities. We are unique, and that's how he loves us.

WHY PURGATORY?

Trees and flowers have wilted and dropped leaves; the colors of fall are fading. As winter draws near perhaps our thoughts as well turn to what's beyond this life. The liturgical year considers this too as we celebrate All Souls' Day on November 2. What happens if we die but aren't in God's grace? If we have sin that stains our souls? No darkness can survive in the glory of God's presence, but are a few blemishes enough to warrant hell? After all, "Who may go up the mountain of the Lord? Who can stand in his holy place? The clean of hand and pure of heart" (Ps. 24:3–4). Those are pretty lofty standards for us mere humans. Yes, we have free will to choose not to sin, but it's in our fallen nature to sin. Even after we're baptized and perhaps make frequent confessions, we still sin. And unless we're fortunate enough to make a worthy last confession, we will most likely die with sins still with us. That kind of blocks us out of the above category: "whose hands are sinless." Thank heavens we have a merciful God who doesn't limit us to heaven or hell! Those who, at death, accept God's love and mercy but aren't yet worthy to see him face to face are cast into purgatory. While it may sound correct to say a soul is going *to* purgatory,

purgatory isn't so much a place as it is a process. According to the *Catechism of the Catholic Church*, imperfectly purified souls "undergo a purification after death," a state in which they are purged of their sins, hence the name purgatory (Catholic Church, 1054).

So where is purgatory mentioned in the Bible? The first mention is found in 2 Maccabees 12:46, "Thus [Judas Maccabeus] made atonement for the dead that they might be freed from this sin." However, this isn't the only place the concept of waiting souls being neither in heaven nor in hell is mentioned. Some scholars believe Jesus could have been referring to purgatory in Matthew 18:21–35, when he mentions an official being handed over to the torturers until all has been paid back, and the Father treating us the same way unless we forgive. There's no coming back from hell, so where are souls to go to pay a debt except purgatory? A place of penance is also implied in Revelation 6:9–11 and more specifically in 1 Peter 3:19. In Peter's letter, after stating that when Christ's body was put to death and his spirit made alive, he wrote, "In it he also went to preach to the spirits in prison."

The question keeps coming up: why need purgatory? I have faith in Christ, I've led a good life, that's enough, isn't it? A little concrete example of purgatory that I like to use is this: Suppose you're at a friend's house and you have an argument. In a fit of rage, you punch a hole in the wall and stomp out. Later you return and apologize (confession). That's wonderful for the relationship, but there's still a hole in the wall. Now you need to repair the hole and clean up the damage (penance). Confession is good for the soul, but doing penance, something to heal the hurt, also brings one closer to God. The two go hand in hand. Penance can also be a very humbling experience, in which one acknowledges that God is God and we are his creation, a good viewpoint to have in heading down a narrow path. This doesn't mean we can err as much as we want in this life and have purgatory as a safety net. According to the saints in their private revelation, doing a little bit of penance in this life can take years off the suffering of purgatory. Why cause our waiting to see God to be longer than needed? Imagine, "What eye has not seen, and ear has not heard, and what has not entered the human heart, what God has prepared for those who love him" (1 Cor. 2:9).

THE NECESSITY OF PRAYER

I was recently speaking with a small group when the question came up on whether or not anyone attended church. One elderly woman kind of huffed and said that going to some church wasn't going to save her. I later discovered that in much younger years, she had attended church, but her father had a falling out with the minister, and they never went back. She seemed rather closed to the idea of ever returning. I was sad—to think of cutting yourself off from God because of misunderstanding with a mortal person. In a sense though, that woman was right: going to church isn't going to save her. Jesus has already done that. What's necessary now is prayer. Jesus told Martha's sister, Mary, she had chosen the better part, to sit and listen to his words (Luke 10:38–42). Our spiritual journey begins in earnest with the desire for more than ourselves and what we can humanly attain, causing us to lift up our souls and search out our Father in heaven. The one who can fulfill our needs will kindly look on us and stretch out his hands and perhaps say, "Finally! Now I can teach you to walk in my way." The Holy Spirit is always there, flickering around our hearts, waiting for that yes to be let in. The degree that he is able to work in us depends on our response. The more we let him, the more God will manifest himself in us. How long has he been waiting for that woman to say, "Are you there, God? It's me." That's all the more he would need to be able to come in and start healing old wounds. But before anyone can begin in prayer, they have to let go of something: pride. Prayer is humble because it admits that there is someone higher than ourselves out there to whom we are willing to listen. Prayer is also a two-way conversation. We talk and Jesus listens. Then we are silent; Jesus talks and we listen. Sometimes it's hard not to forget the being silent part.

My prayer for anyone is that God give them the desire to pray, and they would respond with a yes. How sad to live and not know the joy that comes from loving God! How sad for a soul not to know that it is loved beyond imagining, beyond the faulty love of us humans. Imagine going through your life without knowing Jesus, and then at the end of your life meeting a stranger who turns out to be your

God. How can we then say to someone who is on the threshold of death, "It's okay. This is Jesus. You can go with him now"? I would rather know my God and not be scared at the end of my life! Let us pray for all people everywhere, especially for children, that they come to know the Lord and that their desire is for him. I pray they are so familiar with Jesus that they don't notice the threshold called death and just fall joyfully into his arms. May this be God's will for all people! Blessed be our Father!

GOD OF WONDERS

"Do you really believe all that stuff?" The remark was made when I wondered aloud what our grandma was doing right then. Granny had died two days ago, and my mom and I had been praying our hearts out by her hospital bed. I hoped and prayed that our Lady took her to heaven. Granny wasn't very educated in her faith; she knew the Rosary and Mass and that was about it. But what she had was more important: she knew God with her heart. A week before she died, I asked her if she was scared. Granny said, "No, I'm not scared. I'm Catholic, and I know what's going to happen, so I'm not scared." That's got to count for something.

But I have to wonder how many people have been raised Catholic but not stepped foot inside a church for years? Perhaps they can be told all sorts of things about Jesus, Mary, the saints, and miracles; but to them, they're just words. I don't know what spark it will take to ignite God's fire in their hearts. I can give people prayer cards, but why should they pray to "someone who might be out there?" At one alleged apparition place, the Virgin Mary said to pray until prayer becomes a joy for you, but how does one start praying? For those of us who were raised in the faith and believe, we know God and feel there is a person we're speaking with. We know Christ's story. But what, through all these centuries, has urged unbelieving people to turn away from darkness and look longingly at the light with a desire to pray to a god?

I read a story in *A Memory for Wonders* by Mother Veronica Namoyo Le Goulard, a Poor Clare nun in Africa. She described how she was raised by Communist parents and had no knowledge of God. Yet once at a very young age while watching a sandstorm, she was overwhelmed by its beauty, and although she had no word for God, she knew he was out there (30). Is that simple story it? God's beauty and power are magnified by his creation, and when we finally notice that we are overwhelmed with a sense of awe and gratitude? Gratitude perhaps at realizing that someone bigger than ourselves is out there, and a humbling relief that we are not in charge of the universe. Gratitude that we've an opportunity to share in this beauty. And from that awe and gratitude comes the desire to touch this immeasurable being, this God of wonders and utter our first prayer, saying, "Thank you." Now we can look with trusting eyes to a God who labels himself our Father, and say to him, "Lead me." In gratitude and trust, we now have hope outside of ourselves. That's the hope that comforts us when, at the end of our lives, we can believe that we'll finally be with our creator, our Father in heaven.

Save our souls

A couple of months ago, in the hours before my grandma died, we read the prayers from the *Pieta* book for someone who is dying. I suppose if I had enough faith, then I would trust that when the prayers say the person will go to heaven, they will. No, not me. My curiosity got the better of me, and I wanted to know for sure. I resorted to a novena to the Little Flower, St. Theresa of the Child Jesus. It was a rather trial-and-error experience as I hadn't said a novena like this for a good many years. I knew I was to expect a rose, but exactly when I wasn't sure. During the novena? The day I completed it? I said the novena and nothing happened. I knew I'd forgotten to pray one of the days, so it was my own fault. The same thing happened the next time I said it; for various reasons, I managed to mess it up each time. I was determined one last time to get it right while simultaneously preparing for a resounding silence from heaven. Perhaps I wasn't supposed to receive a rose. This time I was specific too. Laughingly, I said I wanted a real white rose if she was in heaven and a red one if in purgatory. I did the big twenty-four Glory Be novena and finally got the whole thing right. And guess what? I received three real white roses on the seventh day of the novena! God is good!

During my failed novena weeks, God opened my eyes to another need. As I was considering the possibility that Granny was in purgatory, my prayers grew more intense to get her out. I didn't want her to suffer anymore after all she'd gone through here. That's only a natural reaction. I'd always known mentally about the souls in purgatory, but now I knew them in my heart. I wanted them to see God. I wanted their suffering over. It didn't matter that I didn't know for whom specifically I was praying, I just wanted them to see him face to face forever. Suddenly, all those Hail Marys I'd been saying while passing by cemeteries took on new urgent meaning. Yes, I was so happy to receive the roses for Granny, and now I thank God also for letting me know in a new way the suffering souls as well. What about souls who have no one to pray for them? How much we can help those souls through our prayers and sacrifices! Every little annoyance or joy can be a sacrifice—a splinter on your thumb. It doesn't matter. God can take everything and use it in reparation for sins—our own sins and the sins of others. Just as sin affects all people, our reparation affects all people too. When we help each other to reach the heart of God, then we are doing his will. What a wonderful gift to give our Lord: sacrifices for the pure, unselfish hope of getting souls to heaven. It's a gift as well for the person who finally gets to see God face to face. And if we ever need incentive to pray, just remember that someday we could be there too. Wouldn't we want someone to pray for us?

HOLY GROUND

"You write it down for me!" complained my oldest daughter, referring to her book log and homework due. "I want to pack my lunch, not buy!" cried my youngest. All this took place about two minutes after they were supposed to be out waiting for the bus. I also knew I had a half-page long list of things to get done that day. My head was already starting to pound, and I could feel my heart racing. Not a good way to begin a day.

As soon as the girls were on the bus and I finished the dishes, I stopped. I put my list aside. I went into the living room, opened a window, and lay down on the floor beneath it and prayed, "Jesus, calm me down." Looking up, I could see red-and-gold leaves fluttering against a blue sky. A few birds sang, and occasionally, a cloud passed by. When my pulse finally returned to normal, I could listen to what God was saying. No, it wasn't one of those earth-rocking prayer moments, just a quiet time permeated with the Holy Spirit. It left me refreshed and filled with his strength. Now it occurs to me that what I got out of that prayer time applies to us all, so let me share it with you.

God created this beautiful world in which we live. How often do we notice it? Think about it: we surround ourselves with man-made homes, cars, workplaces, etc. When we're outside, we often walk on paved roads and sidewalks. Our feet rub against shoes. How much contact do we have with what God made? When's the last time we took a walk in the woods? He also made us, yet when we talk to each other, are we busy doing other things? Do we stop and give eye contact? Let our hands stop our work and pay attention? The world is holy ground, a palace our Father made for us to live in, and we are temples of his glory. Do we treat each other as such?

Despite all of our pressing matters and emergencies, our things-to-get-done list will only grow. It's a busy world, and we can't do it all. If we take time to pray and remain focused on him, the Holy Spirit will order our day and his will, will take priority. God is bigger than us, and he's bigger than this world we'll leave. What he wants done will find a way of being done. We need to take time to pray no matter where we are or what we're doing. We need to ask our Father to let there be less of us on the inside and more of him. Let him come and annihilate our very being in the furnace of his love, and so let his desires become ours. Then he will walk with us throughout the day, and we'll have a bit of heaven with us here on earth. It will give us that hope we need to get through the day. Then we will not doubt that what we are doing matters, that our washing of windows, done in union with Jesus, is saving as many souls as the nun bowing her head in prayer. Our lives can be holy. Let him transform us.

There's so much more. Go and pray. Let yourself feel him carrying you and don't be anxious. "Be still and confess that I am God!" (Ps. 46:11).

CHOOSING TO PRAISE HIM

Every so often something catches our attention and makes us pause. One thing that captivated me was a simple phrase: "Lift up your hearts!" I was in grade school, and during one Latin Mass (masses were in English, I just think the sisters wanted us to brush up on our Latin once in a while), the priest said, "Sursum corda" and lifted his arms. My gaze continued up above the altar to a risen Christ crucifix. Jesus was extending his arms in blessing, and I remember feeling joy at that moment. I don't know why that phrase stuck with me. Perhaps it was the first time I was conscious of those words, or I was associating the words with the image of the risen Jesus. Whatever it was, it seemed appropriate that we joyfully lift up our hearts to God.

Several years later, in high school, I was at a funeral for a friend who'd died in a car accident. Again the priest said, "Lift up your hearts" and "let us give thanks." I wondered if we should still lift up our hearts at such a time, and need we still give thanks and praise? At that time, my parents were divorcing and all sorts of events were shattering my world. Now I never questioned God's existence or was angry at him (although I suppose that might have been healthy). I just questioned, "Why?" I could understand lifting up my heart in joy and now in sorrow for him to comfort, but to praise him? I wrestled with this concept. How could I praise God when all these horrible things happen? I had latched onto an enduring question of humanity.

An answer that I could live with came slowly. As I lifted up my heart to Jesus, I recognized that his tears mixed with mine. Every one of us, young and old, were his children, and he cried over our brokenness. Death and divorce weren't his idea. Then I grappled with evil and sin in the world and our free will. I saw how wondrous our God was, who, in his strength, gave us the choice of praising him. We could choose to love or reject the very God who made us. He could desire us, but he would not force us. Therefore, the very act of raising our hearts to him, whatever their state, becomes a blessing to him. How beautiful that thought was to me. If I imagined our hearts as altars, then in our joyful, abundant times, we raised up altars bursting with flowers and songs of praise. On the opposite end, in those times when we have been stripped of everything and have nothing left to offer—perhaps just a void of emotion and thought—then Jesus himself will come to our bare altars and adorn them with his own wounds. Then we can still give him thanks and praise for allowing us to share in his passion. It's as I consider the compassion and greatness of our God that I know even more his magnitude, and yet in all of our days, we will never comprehend him. What better reason than that can we have to lift up our hearts to our Father who knows us inside and out? Everything we have comes from him, so let us joyfully return to God what is already his. Sursum corda!

Praying always

> Some see prayer as a flight from the world in a reaction against activism, but in fact, Christian prayer is neither an escape from reality nor a divorce from life.
>
> —Catholic Church

We are so busy these days with so many different activities. We aren't seen as productive if we're not visibly accomplishing something. But where is all this busyness getting us? Is it actively getting us closer to heaven, or is it the devil's conspiring to take us further from God? Prayer—our relationship with God—is the main thing our daily lives should be centered on, yet prayer is often viewed as unproductive because we cannot see spiritual realities. Some say, "I'm too busy to pray," or "if my life were perfect, I'd have time to pray." What

Archbishop Fulton Sheen said about virtue could easily be applied to prayer: "There are many who excuse themselves, saying that if they were in other circumstances they would be much more patient. This is a grave mistake, for it assumes that virtue is a matter of geography and not on moral effort. It makes little difference where we are; it all depends on what we are thinking about" (Benkovic 2003, 156).

We pretty much choose how busy we want our lives to be, and whatever the circumstances, sometimes the grass will look greener on the other side. We need to commit ourselves to taking time to pray at certain times, even if it's just one thought, because then we'll remember to pray spontaneously as well. "We cannot pray 'at all times' if we do not pray at specific times, consciously willing it. These are special times of Christian prayer, both in intensity and duration" (Catholic Church, 2697). Whether it's going to Mass, grace before meals, prayer before bed, etc., if we get used to saying set prayers, then it will be more natural to offer up more prayer throughout the day. As we go from one activity to the next, we can ask Jesus to accompany us and guide us or to use it for his intentions or to gain grace for us. This is how we pray at all times. Not by necessarily kneeling and bowing our head and repeating formal prayers—although sometimes that's easier—and we *feel* more like we're praying, but by asking our Lord to be with us throughout the day. We ask him to help us make decisions, to take a walk with us as we relax, guide us as we relate to others, laugh and cry with us, and just talk to him as we share our hopes and dreams. "Prayer is a remembrance of God often awakened by the memory of the heart" (Catholic Church, 2697). When we remember God, we start to be concerned with what he's thinking and about how we live our lives, and then our lives change. Prayer isn't as complex as we make it. The more we think of God, the more we're drawn to him, and that "being drawn" is prayer. It can happen any time, even now.

AN ATTITUDE OF GRATITUDE

Even though Thanksgiving isn't a religious holiday, what a better time to consider our blessings and all God has given us, good and bad. We need to thank him as the action and feeling remind us that we are only creatures gratefully indebted to our creator. In order to have a sense of who we are, in order to be kind, we must have humility.

Once when I was considering the holidays from a child's point of view and then a parent's, I caught a glimpse of how God must be blessed by our gratitude. A child is awed by the sights, smells, and sounds of Thanksgiving and Christmas. She enjoys eating the food, opening the presents, and playing with them, oblivious to the behind-the-scenes work. As parents, we provide the sights, smells, sounds, and gifts. We know the work and effort that went into the season and the whole experience. So when we see our kids enjoying the day with its food, tree lights, and toys, we are pleased. We're even more flattered when our kids think to say thank you for things. In other words, when we see our kids happy and grateful, we are blessed. What a gift! Now, let's apply this to us and God. God is our Father, we are his children. Our Father does an awful lot of work for us; things which we have no clue how to fathom. Sometimes we see the results of his work, a beautiful day, good times with family and friends, or a good day at work, and we are pleased. Do we stop to whisper in our hearts, "Thank you"? When we do, do we consider that God is pleased, even blessed, by us in our gratitude? What a gift to give that we can bless God. Gratitude is a wonderful thing because with it comes humility. If we are grateful, then we are acknowledging that someone's done something for us, and we owe them a debt. Pride has no room for gratitude.

What about all the things in our lives which, to most eyes, don't deserve gratitude? What about the natural and manmade disasters? What about the poverty and disease, and in a smaller sense, the daily, minor setbacks? I can't see the whole picture of God's plan here on earth. "For my thoughts are not your thoughts, nor are your ways my ways, says the Lord" (Isa. 55:8). I also "know that all things work for good for those who love God" (Rom. 8:28). Being grateful to our Father in those times, foolish to the world as it may be, is a matter of faith. Here I will redouble my efforts when I have to say, "The Lord gave and the Lord has taken away; blessed be the name of the Lord!" (Job 1:21).

Personally, I want my Father to see that I'm happy and grateful for what he's given me. If my saying thank you pleases and blesses him, then what better gift can I offer?

Blessings without number

> We ought to give thanks for all fortune: if it is "good,"
> because it is good, if "bad" because it works in us
> patience, humility and the contempt of this world
> and the hope of our eternal country.

—C. S. Lewis, letter to Don Giovanni Calabria

Sometimes a blessing is so commonplace, we forget to give thanks for it. We need something to open our eyes and make us realize what it is we have, but unfortunately, not until that blessing is taken away do we miss it and regret that we took it for granted. I'm thinking in particular of our country and our government.

I know a lot of complaining is going on right now about particular people in office, but this isn't to voice a complaint. Rather, it's to point out how wonderful it is that we can complain, crazy as it sounds. Freedom of speech, press, religion, petitioning the government, and assembly are guaranteed in the First Amendment, and we need to take care lest they are eroded away. We in America are spoiled by our blessings and don't value them. Just look at other countries. In 1992, in Russia, after I was at a Mass in a hotel conference room, the manager commented that this would never have happened a couple years ago. Their government had finally relaxed some prohibitions. Later, I was helping at a Bible study in a lot outside our building. People of all ages, children to elderly, were there, and they were excited to be there. One old lady with a scarf on her head kept raising her hand to answer questions, bouncing like a kid in school. In the US, we don't need permission to gather for a Bible study, we just announce it and then have to convince people to come. Perhaps because our freedoms and blessings are so commonplace, they've become less precious to us.

An activity that might help us be more aware of our blessings could be simply writing them down. Start at the beginning of our day and write down everything that we do and find the blessings of freedom in it. What about private conversations? After friends were questioned by a KGB official about something said in our hotel room, I'll never take private conversations for granted again. Do we have food on the table? Did we even worry about having enough? Write down the people in our life; they are blessings too, even the ones we don't like, because they make us grow in grace. Did we write down the soldiers who gave us our freedom that we enjoy? Then thank God for every blessing he's given us, and thank God we live in America while we're at it. If we don't thank him but expect to keep on receiving, we might be seen as ungrateful. Personally, I don't know if God would ever revoke a blessing (like a parent revoking privileges), but I know I don't want to see what would happen if he did. What we have is precious, and it's worth speaking up for lest it slip away. And always, with grateful hearts, give thanks.

When America worships God, God will bless America.

Faith under fire

> O God, we praise You, and acknowledge You to be the supreme Lord. Everlasting Father, all the earth worships You.

> (Te Deum 2014)

How glorious these words of the Te Deum rang out in the cathedral in Vladimir, Russia. I had the wonderful opportunity of observing a solemn Mass on one of my visits. I had been to orthodox masses before, but that day the deep male voices, the incense, and the gonging bells insisted that God be worshipped in his holiness. How fervent were they in their worship? After people made the sign of the cross they bent at the waist, touching the floor with their fingers, a small, humble prostration before their Lord.

Upon returning to America, the culture shock was acute. I thanked God every day that I was American, yet part of me longed for the intensity of faith I found in the old Soviet Union. As I considered the differences between the two countries, the reasons became clearer as to why the varied responses to religion. Not to say that one is better than the other, but there are lessons to be learned from both. For years, the Russian people were oppressed under a Communist regime. To be found practicing religion meant imprisonment or death. Icons were hidden behind pictures of Lenin. Even just a couple years ago, the mother of a Russian friend of mine never practiced her faith because she would have lost her job. Still, it was through the fire of suffering that their faith was strengthened. They had to hold on to God tightly or he would have been stripped from them, just as their churches were stripped and made into state museums. Here in America, we don't have to hold on so tightly. We wake up on Sunday mornings and complain about going to Mass, even though we can attend in open, obvious church buildings without worrying about Big Brother noticing. We are free to witness Christ by bumper stickers, T-shirts, newsletters, you name it, and we can do it. We don't take advantage of many opportunities like daily Mass, confession, fasting. My Russian friend was surprised to learn that as a norm, we Catholics don't fast here in America. "Why not?" she said. "You can." Yes, we can. And perhaps because we can worship God so easily without fearing for our lives, we've let those practices go. Not only are we letting them go, we seem to be pushing them out the door. We take away any mention of God in our schools, so our children can't learn about him, and we secularize our holidays. In the name of religious freedom, we forbid prayer before sporting events. God gives us so many freedoms in this country, even the freedom to say, "We don't want you in our lives." Now we are reaping the fruits of that freedom. Just look at the moral decay of our society and the values we embrace. We can't complain too much; they're what we've sown.

Perhaps, as our holiday of Thanksgiving draws near, we shouldn't just let it be one day. We have the opportunity to give him thanks every day. Let's not buy into the explanations of how God will be taken away next, but let's work to bring him back. Then we too can sing "You are God. We praise you!" with passionate enthusiasm and truly thank him for our freedoms.

GOING HOME

"If I find in myself a desire which no experience in this world can satisfy, the most probable explanation is that I was made for another world"

(Martindale and Root 1989, 287)

I love going home to visit. Home for me, my first home that is, is on the banks of the Mississippi River. I'd spent my whole life there until after college when I moved to Meadville. Now Meadville is home as well, but I love heading back to the old "Muddy Mississip." I can start to smell the river before I can see it. A little farther, and bluffs start to trumpet up from the ground and break the paper flatness of the prairie. Up close, the river washes over the limestone rocks, and barges push their way through water too thin to plow and too thick to drink. And there's nothing like sitting up high on the bluffs, watching the white line of a thunderstorm coming down the river, and feeling the wind picking up. I suppose the Mississippi has done a good job of winding its way into my heart. The funny thing is that whether I'm away from the river and the nostalgia can practically knock me over or whether I'm there and basking in the delight of being home, I'm not satisfied; I'm still yearning for something. I remind myself that I won't be satisfied until I finally reach my true home, and God will completely saturate my being. I ache because I want him only, and I want everyone to know him and they don't, and they can't seem to share that joy of loving God with me. Again I remind myself that as much as I long for home when I'm away, that is nothing compared to the ache for heaven that God has placed in me, and I am delighted that he has done it. It tells me that as much as I yearn for him, that's a mere shadow of how He longs for me. And I will be forever and ever grateful to our God for giving up his Son so that we can come home. Thank you, Jesus, for being the key to open the gate of heaven for us. Thank you for making right what we messed up and for setting us on the right path again. Thank you for loving us. Help us to love you back. Help me to never be ungrateful for the gift you've given.

Someday I'll get there, but not until he says. Till then, I'll have to stay here and do whatever it is he's given me to do. Some days that's easier to figure out than others. At this minute, what I'm supposed to do is share with you that God exists. He loves you and is waiting for you at home. Remember that whatever nostalgia you feel for anything on this earth is nothing compared to what's waiting for you in heaven. I also happen to know there's a river waiting for me up there too because he told me so. (Rev. 22:1–2)

Follow the map

I like to know where I'm going. Don't most of us? There are times in life when decisions come up, we ask God for help and we'd like clear answers. I'd like mine in skywriting or neon signs. When life gets all muddled up and we can't see above the waves, we start to panic or get anxious and depressed because we don't know how we'll pull through or which way to go. That's when we need to remember that we are Christians and God's laid out his whole plan for us. Our creed is God's plan of salvation history, but do we pay attention to what it says? We know the beginning, creation, and the focal point, which was Jesus's death and resurrection. Now we celebrate that focal point in the Mass and the Eucharist, but how often do we go to communion, follow the commandments, and try to live the way Jesus taught us just because it's what he told us to do? Do we forget why we're doing it all? It can't be just habit. It's too hard to live that way just because someone told us to long ago. Let's not forget the little phrase in the creed, "And he will come again in glory." That's where we're going as well—to be with him in glory. We need to live our lives in a sense of expectation. Sometimes we're so caught up in the past, in what Jesus did that we forget what he's still doing. The plan isn't finished yet. Jesus said he will come, and he will. We don't need to be fearful of his return; in his mercy, God the Father hid the time of return from us, but we ought to be joyful at the prospect. "When Christ your life appears, then you too will appear with him in glory" (Col. 3:4). It's not just us struggling along here on earth by ourselves (again, remember the whole plan). The church includes those in purgatory and heaven. Our family and friends in heaven pray for us. We can't forget to pray for the souls in purgatory and to make reparation for our own sins. Life is so short. Knowing that, surely, we have the courage to offer up whatever trial we currently face. We should "consider it all joy, my brothers, when you encounter various trials, for you know that the testing of your faith produces perseverance" (James 1:2–3). That endurance is backed by the hope that we have in our confession of faith. If we aren't hoping for eternal life with the Trinity in heaven, then why try to live as Jesus said? What do we have to hold on to during those moments of life when we're just not sure we're going to make it through? And knowing that eternal life is what my Father in heaven desires for my family and me as well, I can breathe a little easier. No, my salvation doesn't depend on me. All I have to do is pray, love my Lord, and do my best to translate that love to the people around me. This is the communion of saints: God's children who are on their way to heaven helping each other to get there too. This is our confession of faith, our hope that Jesus gave his life for, that we would someday be one in the Trinity. Surely, this is our encouragement to get through life's worst struggles. After all, Jesus us waiting for us.

THANK YOU

Have you ever given someone a gift and then discovered that the gift was never used? What if you gave the same person a variety of gifts year after year, trying to match their interests and putting a lot of thought into them, and then found the gifts were never redeemed, never used? Ouch. That would hurt. It would also be discouraging. You might begin to wonder if that person cares for you at all or is horrendously thoughtless, or just what is the message the person it trying to send? Eventually, you might learn to live with disappointment, letting the tears fall hidden. The sensible thing to do would be to stop giving gifts, but what if you loved that person and wanted to do something to show you loved them anyway and were just a glutton for punishment?

What if you discovered the person was you?

When we realize our Father in heaven is showering us with gifts, hopefully, we are grateful. We usually at least remember to say thank you and may even try to make some return to show our gratitude. But what if we simply take our gifts for granted, expecting God to provide them and never bother to say thanks? Our Father has given us everything from supernatural gifts for building up his church to everyday gifts like food, clothing, and shelter, not to mention, he gave us our life. He gave them to us because he loves us. For some strange reason, he still loves us despite all the hurt we inflict. He loves us enough to die for us and gave us the Eucharist. To be the recipients of such gifts! And yet there are some who would deny him, who would deny that all the things they have are anything but their own hard work. How it tears at his heart! How his tears fall at our lack of love. Has anyone ever come with his heart in his hands to a people as rebellious as we? Those of us who love the Lord, who recognize his gifts for what they are, need to make up for the hardness of those who don't know. If we have love in our hearts then we want everyone to know God's love. We need to make reparation for the wounds he wears because of us. Can any of us bear to see the ones we love hurt or slighted in any way? We want to comfort them. Maybe God, being God, doesn't really need our comfort, but he sees that we are growing when we think of others beyond ourselves and are learning a lesson.

Let's not send an apathetic message of uncaring to our Father who loves us so much. Next time we notice a gift we've been given, let's say "thank you" and put it to good use.

COMING FULL CIRCLE

The liturgical year ends with the celebration of Christ the King, when we look forward to his second coming in glory. How different will it be, his first and second coming? Two thousand years ago, Jesus came at Christmas to a little town named Bethlehem, meaning "house of bread." A star shone out his light to those willing to see it, and they came in adoration. What grace was given to those people? Were their lives changed because they had looked in wonder at the face of God? Today, we have our own houses of bread, our churches, where Jesus resides in the tabernacle. In our faith, can we see the radiance of his Eucharistic presence? Do we allow it to draw us in adoration to the Holy Hours? Our Eucharistic Lord is the life of every parish. Do we acknowledge that? "O my people, what have I done to you, or how have I wearied you?" (Mic. 6:3).

Let's renew our efforts again to find that tiny whispering voice of Jesus in our hearts. Let us quiet our spirits so that instead of reflecting the world around us, we can say with Mary. "My soul proclaims the greatness of the Lord; my spirit rejoices in God my savior" (Luke 1:46–47). Every holy hour, every Mass can be that first Christmas again. May we find joy in being before the Blessed Sacrament and love filling our hearts. May we, with Mary and Joseph, kneel in silent wonder and pray, "O come, let us adore him."

I love spending time in adoration before the Eucharist, but rare are the times when I can express what I'm feeling in my heart. One of those times came at the beginning of Advent during a Festival of Praise at Franciscan University in Steubenville, Ohio. A festival is simply two hours of singing and praising God accompanied by the workings of the Holy Spirit. When the Blessed Sacrament was brought out, how can I describe the enthusiasm that filled the field house? Jesus could have been no more present than if he had split the heavens and come crashing through the roof to be on that altar. The same Jesus who had walked with his friends over the dusty hills of Nazareth so long ago had come, and he received a king's welcome. Christmas songs sung in the presence of our Lord took on new meaning: "O come let us adore him…" And then, songs of pure love: "Beautiful one, I love you! Beautiful one, I adore! Beautiful one, my soul must sing!" (Camp 2004, track 2). Truly, our souls had to sing. How can mere words express what filled our hearts that night? What can explain that one of the priests on the altar, hands clasped, and eyes shining, fell on his knees before the Eucharist other than love? One priest then processed the monstrance through the crowd.

Imagine the woman who reached out to touch Jesus as he passed, hoping for healing. Now we were that close. Imagine Jesus still healing as he passed by, raised in blessing, being blessed. Jesus, receiving praise and honor in the "Tantum ergo" and the joyful longing in our hearts as he left. What a gift we had received! And to think that same Jesus waits in our churches every day.

Does all this sound a bit hyped up? A tad too emotional? It's okay. Jesus's coming among us was real. It was as real as a touchdown at a football game or a concert where the crowds go wild. Society doesn't look on those people as fanatical. So are we, as Christians, not supposed to show any emotion when our *God* comes among us? Yet the ways of God are folly in men's eyes. We must give as a gift what we have been given: the joy of knowing that Jesus's coming means our freedom. By his blood, he has forgiven us our sins and death has no more hold on us. It is our duty to live in the deep-rooted joy of Christ, to be his reflection and shine out in the darkness. Jesus has been born in our hearts. Come, Christ the King!

With the end of November, we have come full circle. We welcome Christ as our end, anticipating our union with him in glory. Throughout the year, we've traveled with Mary, Joseph, and Jesus, participating in the mystery and sharing in the joy, grief, and wonder of God becoming human. Even as much as we think we know Jesus's whole story, we've seen but a glimpse of a monumental plan. Our Father knows the deepest needs of our hearts and has moved heaven and earth so he could reach down to us, lift us up, and gently ask, "Do you see what I've done for you?" Each of us has an irreplaceable part in this story. I've shared my little piece with you, hoping you will find inspiration and encouragement along your way. Don't give up. He's waiting for you, calling you. May we find the courage to lift our arms to our Father, our majestic king, and respond, saying, "What do you want me to do for you?"

REFERENCES

Benedict XVI. 2008. "Votive Mass for the Universal Church." The Holy See Online. Accessed April 2014. http://www.vatican.va/holy_father/benedict_xvi/homilies/2008/documents/hf_ben-xvi_hom_20080419_st-patrick-ny_en.html.

Benkovic, Johnnette. 2003. *Experience grace in abundance: Ten strategies for your spiritual life.* Huntington, Our Sunday Visitor Publishing Division.

Camp, Jeremey. 2004. "Beautiful One." *Carried Me: The Worship Project.* CD. Seattle, BEC Recordings.

Catholic Church. 1976. *Christian Prayer: The Liturgy of the Hours.* New York: Catholic Book Publishing Co.

Catholic Church. 1994. *Catechism of the Catholic Church.* Vatican: Libreria editrice Vaticana.

Catholics against Contraception. 2001. *The Holy Rosary.* http://www.catholicsagainstcontraception.com/rosary.html.

Chesterton, G.K. 1919. *Heretics.* Project Gutenberg. Accessed March 2014. http://www.gutenberg.org/ebook/470

Demaray, Donald. 1992. *The Little Flowers of St. Francis: A Paraphrase.* New York: Alba House.

Forward Boldly. 2011. "On Redemptive Suffering." Laudem Gloriae (blog). Accessed March 2014. http://laudemgloriae.blogspot.com/2011/12/on-redemptive-suffering.html.

Franciscan Friars of the Immaculate. 1997. *A Handbook on Guadalupe.* New Bedford: Franciscan Friars of the Immaculate.

Heilman, Rick. 2011. "Heaven's weapon–the Rosary." Knights of the Divine Mercy website. Accessed May 2014. http://www.knightsofdivinemercy.com/2011/04/07/heaven%E2%80%99s-weapon-%E2%80%93-the-rosary/

John Paul II. 1981. *Laborem Exercens.* 4-2014. The Holy See Online. http://www.vatican.va/holy_father/john_paul_ii/encyclicals/documents/hf_jp- ii_enc_14091981_laborem-exercens_en.html.

John Paul II. 1994. "Regina Coeli address." The Holy See Online. Accessed April 2014. http://www.vat-ican.va/holy_father/john_paul_ii/angelus/1994/documents/hf_jp-ii_reg_19940424_it.html.

John Paul II. 2001. *Novo Millennio Ineunte.* The Holy See Online. Accessed April 2014. http://www.vatican.va/holy_father/john_paul_ii/apost_letters/documents/hf_jp-ii_apl_20010106_novo-millennio-ineunte_en.html.

John Paul II. 2002. *Rosarium Virginis Mariae.* 3-2014. The Holy See Online. http://www.vatican.va/holy_father/john_paul_ii/apost_letters/documents/hf_jp- ii_apl_20021016_rosarium-virginis-mariae_en.html.

John Paul II. 2002. "World Day of Peace." The Holy See Online. Accessed March 2014. http://www.vatican.va/holy_father/john_paul_ii/messages/peace/documents/hf_jp-ii_mes_20011211_xxxv-world-day-for-peace_en.html.

John Paul II. 2002. "Address of John Paul II to a Delegation of Members of the Renewal in the Holy Spirit Movement." The Holy See Online. Accessed March 2014. http://www.vatican.

va/holy_father/john_paul_ii/speeches/2002/march/documents/
hf_jp-ii_spe_20020314_rinnovamento-spirito-santo_en.html.

John Paul II. 2004. *Homily.* 4-2014. The Holy See Online. http://
www.vatican.va/holy_father/john_paul_ii/homilies/2004/
documents/hf_jp-ii_hom_20040529_vigil-pentecost_en.html.

Keucher, Mike. 2010. "Mother Teresa and the rosary." The Long
Journey into Light. Blog. Accessed May 2014. http://tallsemi-
narian.blogspot.com/2010/10/mother-teresa-and- rosary.html.

Kiefer, James. n.d. "Dame Julian of Norwich, Contemplative."
Biographical Sketches of Memorable Christians
of the Past. Accessed March 2014. http://jus-
tus.anglican.org/resources/bio/154.html.

Kowalska, Faustina. 1990. *Diary of Sister M. Faustina
Kowalska.* Stockbridge: Marian Press.

Le Goulard, Veronica. P.C.C., V. (1993). *A Memory for
Wonders: A True Story.* San Francisco: Ignatius Press.

Lewis, Clive S. 1970. *The Hose and His Boy.* New
York: Macmillan Publishing Co.

Lombardi, Esther. 2014. "Moby Dick Quotes." Accessed
April 2014. http://classiclit.about.com/od/moby-
dickhermanmelville/a/aa_mobydickqu.html.

Lucia, Martin. 1984. *Rosary Meditations from Mother Teresa of
Calcutta.* Mt. Clemens: Apostolate of Perpetual Adoration.

Martindale, Wayne and Root, Jerry, ed. 1989. *The Quotable
Lewis.* Wheaton: Tyndale House Publishers, Inc.

Mastrorilli, Maurizio. 2003. *Order of the Poor Sisters of Saint
Clare of Assisi.* Accessed April 2014. http://www.rilievo.
poliba.it/bsc/bsc/st/cc/orm/francescani/index.html

McCarthy, Andrew. 2010. *Francis of Assisi as Artist of the Spiritual Life: An Object Relations Theory Perspective.* Lanham: University Press of America.

Moore, Christopher. 2012. "A New Pentecost for a New Evangelization." Accessed March 2014 http://christopherjmoorewriter.wordpress.com.

Mother Teresa. 1983. *Words to Love By.* Notre Dame: Ave Maria Press.

Mother Teresa. 1996. *Mother Teresa: Meditations from a Simple Path.* Compiled by Lucinda Vardey. New York: Ballantine Books.

Mother Teresa. 2007. *Mother Teresa: Come Be My Light.* Edited by Brian Kolodiejchuk. New York: Random House.

Paul VI. 1965. Vatican II *Apostolica Actuositatem.* The Holy See Online.

Pio. 2003. *Secrets of a Soul.* Edited by Elvira G. DiFabio. Boston: Pauline Books & Media.

Priests of the Sacred Heart. n.d. *Daily Prayers.* Hales Corners: Sacred Heart Monastery.

Saint-Exupery, Antoine de. 1943. *The Little Prince.* New York: Harcourt.

Siena, Catherine. 1995. "Saint Catherine of Siena: Do for Your Neighbor What You Cannot Do For Me." *Houston Catholic Worker.* Accessed on March 2014. http://cjd.org/1995/10/01/saint-catherine-of-siena-do-for-your-neighbor-what-you-cannot-do-for-me/.

Silverstein, Shel. 1964. *The Giving Tree.* New York: Harper & Row, Pub.

Straub, Steve. 2011. "John Adams, Letter to Zabdiel Adams (21 June 1776)." 4-2014. http://www. thefederalistpapers.org/founders/adams/ john-adams- letter-to-zabdiel-adams-21-june-1776.

"Suffering and the Cross." n.d. The Feast of All Saints. Accessed March 2014. http://feastofsaints.com/sufferingcross.htm.

Tice, R. Stewart. n.d. "Pray to End Abortion." Pro-Life for Good. Accessed March 2014. http://www.prolifeforgood.net/.

Tucciarone, Tracy. "15 Prayers of St. Bridget of Sweden." Accessed March 2014. http://www.fis-heaters.com/15prayersofstbridget.html.

VanBuskirk, John. 2010 *Kids, It's Time We Have the Talk*. Bloomington, AuthorHouse.

ABOUT THE AUTHOR

Amy Mosbacher has a gift for taking daily life experiences and finding the spiritual, the touch of God in them and helping others to see these touches as well. "I've traveled many places and find God everywhere, whether it's discovering icons behinds pictures of Lenin in Russia or simply being handed a cup of cold well water in a peasant village. Sometimes finding God in the first-world countries is more challenging, but if I can help anyone to see Him then I'm doing my job." Helping people to experience spirit-filled relationships with Jesus drives her activity. Working with children with mental health diagnoses in the public school system, Amy gently presents Christ through her actions to a secular world. She also teaches 11th grade catechetics as well as volunteering in various ministries in her parish and community. Amy grew up along the banks of the Mississippi River in southern Illinois and currently resides in northwestern Pennsylvania with her husband and two daughters.

CPSIA information can be obtained at www.ICGtesting.com
Printed in the USA
LVOW07s1607071015

457323LV00001B/262/P